THE SERMON ON THE MOUNT

THE SERMON ON THE MOUNT

BY
WM. HENDRIKSEN, Th. B.

Author of
"The Covenant of Grace"

WIPF & STOCK · Eugene, Oregon

Wipf and Stock Publishers
199 W 8th Ave, Suite 3
Eugene, OR 97401

The Sermon on the Mount
By Hendriksen, William
Softcover ISBN-13: 978-1-7252-6558-5
Hardcover ISBN-13: 978-1-7252-6560-8
eBook ISBN-13: 978-1-7252-6559-2
Publication date 2/4/2020
Previously published by Eerdmans, 1934

FOREWORD

THIS book contains the *Bible Study Outlines* which appeared in the *Federation Messenger*, vol. iv, from September, 1932, to March, 1933. Together they form a *Commentary* on *The Sermon on the Mount*. Some of the material published in this book did not appear in the Outlines. The most important additions which were made are these two: a discussion of the *paradoxical character* of the beatitudes, Chapter III, *I, C*, and a detailed exegesis of Matthew 5:32, dealing with *divorce*, Chapter IX, *II, B* and Appendix. Several minor changes (mostly additions) have been made in nearly every chapter.

It was the purpose of the author:

a. To *explain* every passage of the Sermon. Although as a rule we have purposely omitted the Greek text, it will be evident that we have tried to make a close study of the original.

b. To *outline* every passage or logical unit, so that the theme and divisions of every paragraph are given. Hence, our treatment of the Sermon is synthetic as well as analytic. We have tried to point out the train of thought, the logical connection, between the verses. As a result we hope that the unity of the entire Sermon will stand out more clearly.

c. To *arrange* the material in such a manner that it may be used with advantage in Bible classes, societies, etc. If a sufficient amount of study in advance is done by the members of a class or of a society, then the Outline can usually be covered at one meeting. *Questions for Discussion* and *Reading and Study Helps* have been added in order to stimulate the interest in the lesson.

We take this opportunity to thank our leaders, editors, etc., for the favorable comments which have been published from time to time ever since the first Outlines appeared in print. It was not without a degree of hesitancy that we took this work upon us. Yet we did not dare to refuse. If a measure of success has accompanied our humble efforts, this must be attributed to the fine spirit of co-operation which characterizes our societies and their leaders.

We also wish to express our gratitude to the Executive Committee of the National Federation of Reformed Men's Societies. Its co-operation has been exemplary. The editor-in-chief of the *Federation Messenger* (the Rev. J. De Haan, Jr.) has assisted us with valuable advice from the beginning and has shown his special interest throughout.

We also wish to acknowledge our special indebtedness to the Rev. Prof. C. Bouma, Th. D., who suggested that we write the Bible Study Outlines; and to the Rev. J. H. Bruinooge, Th. D., for placing in our hands a few very valuable sources.

Last but not least, our own Men's Society (i. e. of the Allen Ave. Christian Reformed Church, Muskegon, Mich.) deserves a word of praise. Its membership has doubled during the season, and the members have given us every encouragement to continue the work.

May the *Gospel of the Kingdom* find a hearty response in the lives of all! Then the *King* who proclaimed this Gospel will be glorified!

W. HENDRIKSEN.

Muskegon, Mich.
April 7, 1933.

CONTENTS

CHAPTER		PAGE
I.	INTRODUCTION	19
	Matthew 5:1, 2.	
	OUTLINE OF THE SERMON ON THE MOUNT:	
II.	THE GOSPEL OF THE KINGDOM	28
III.	I. THE CITIZENS OF THE KINGDOM	37
	THEIR CHARACTER AND BLESSEDNESS (1) Matthew 5:3-5.	
IV.	I. THE CITIZENS OF THE KINGDOM	50
	THEIR CHARACTER AND BLESSEDNESS (2) Matthew 5:6-12.	
V.	I. THE CITIZENS OF THE KINGDOM	60
	THEIR RELATION TO THE WORLD. Matthew 5:13-16.	
VI.	II. THE RIGHTEOUSNESS OF THE KINGDOM	70
	IN HARMONY WITH THE LAW. Matthew 5:17-19.	
VII.	II. THE RIGHTEOUSNESS OF THE KINGDOM	78
	VERSUS THE TRADITIONAL JEWISH INTERPRETATION OF THE LAW. A. *Jesus and the Pharisees.* Matthew 5:20.	
VIII.	II. THE RIGHTEOUSNESS OF THE KINGDOM	85
	VERSUS THE TRADITIONAL JEWISH INTERPRETATION OF THE LAW. B. *The Sixth Commandment.* Matthew 5:21-26.	
IX.	II. THE RIGHTEOUSNESS OF THE KINGDOM	91
	VERSUS THE TRADITIONAL JEWISH INTERPRETATION OF THE LAW. C. *The Seventh Commandment.* Matthew 5:27-32.	
X.	II. THE RIGHTEOUSNESS OF THE KINGDOM	101
	VERSUS THE TRADITIONAL JEWISH INTERPRETATION OF THE LAW. D. *The Third Commandment.* Matthew 5:33-37.	

CHAPTER		PAGE
XI.	II. THE RIGHTEOUSNESS OF THE KINGDOM	108
	VERSUS THE TRADITIONAL JEWISH INTERPRETATION OF THE LAW. E. *The Law of Retaliation.* Matthew 5:38-42.	
XII.	II. THE RIGHTEOUSNESS OF THE KINGDOM	116
	VERSUS THE TRADITIONAL JEWISH INTERPRETATION OF THE LAW. F. *Love Toward the Neighbor.*	
XIII.	II. THE RIGHTEOUSNESS OF THE KINGDOM	123
	ITS ESSENCE WITH RESPECT TO OUR RELATION TO GOD: *The Secret Devotion of the Heart. Illustrated with respect to* A. *Alms-Giving.* Matthew 6:1-4.	
XIV.	II. THE RIGHTEOUSNESS OF THE KINGDOM	129
	ITS ESSENCE WITH RESPECT TO OUR RELATION TO GOD: *The Secret Devotion of the Heart. Illustrated with respect to* B. *Prayer.* Matthew 6:5-8.	
XV.	II. THE RIGHTEOUSNESS OF THE KINGDOM	136
	ITS ESSENCE WITH RESPECT TO OUR RELATION TO GOD: *The Secret Devotion of the Heart. Illustrated with respect to* C. *The Lord's Prayer* (1). Matthew 6:9, 10.	
XVI.	II. THE RIGHTEOUSNESS OF THE KINGDOM	142
	ITS ESSENCE WITH RESPECT TO OUR RELATION TO GOD: *The Secret Devotion of the Heart. Illustrated with respect to* C. *The Lord's Prayer* (2). Matthew 6:11-15.	
XVII.	II. THE RIGHTEOUSNESS OF THE KINGDOM	150
	ITS ESSENCE WITH RESPECT TO OUR RELATION TO GOD: *The Secret Devotion of the Heart. Illustrated with respect to* D. *Fasting.* Matthew 6:16-18.	
XVIII.	II. THE RIGHTEOUSNESS OF THE KINGDOM	156
	ITS ESSENCE WITH RESPECT TO OUR RELATION TO GOD: *Undivided Trust in God*	

CHAPTER		PAGE
	A. *Trust in God versus Mammon-Worship.* Matthew 6:19-24.	
XIX.	II. THE RIGHTEOUSNESS OF THE KINGDOM	162
	ITS ESSENCE WITH RESPECT TO OUR RELATION TO GOD: *Undivided Trust in God* B. *Trust in God versus Worry.* Matthew 6:25-32.	
XX.	II. THE RIGHTEOUSNESS OF THE KINGDOM	172
	ITS ESSENCE WITH RESPECT TO OUR RELATION TO GOD: *Undivided Trust in God* C. *Trust in God Based on God's Promises.* Matthew 6:33, 34.	
XXI.	II. THE RIGHTEOUSNESS OF THE KINGDOM	180
	ITS ESSENCE WITH RESPECT TO OUR RELATION TO MAN: A. *The Absence of a Censorious Attitude.* Matthew 7:1-5.	
XXII.	II. THE RIGHTEOUSNESS OF THE KINGDOM	189
	ITS ESSENCE WITH RESPECT TO OUR RELATION TO MAN: B. *Discrimination in Judgment* (1). Matthew 7:6.	
XXIII.	II. THE RIGHTEOUSNESS OF THE KINGDOM	194
	ITS ESSENCE WITH RESPECT TO OUR RELATION TO MAN: B. *Discrimination in Judgment* (2). *Wisdom to Judge Aright Obtained by Prayer.* Matthew 7:7-11.	
XXIV.	II. THE RIGHTEOUSNESS OF THE KINGDOM	201
	ITS ESSENCE WITH RESPECT TO OUR RELATION TO MAN: C. *The Golden Rule.* Matthew 7:12.	
XXV.	III. EXHORTATION TO ENTER THE KINGDOM	210
	THE BEGINNING OF THE WAY. Matthew 7:13, 14.	
XXVI.	III. EXHORTATION TO ENTER THE KINGDOM	220
	PROGRESS UPON THE WAY. Matthew 7:15-20.	

CHAPTER		PAGE
XXVII.	III. EXHORTATION TO ENTER THE KINGDOM	226
	THE END OF THE WAY. *Sayers versus Doers.* Matthew 7:21-23.	
XXVIII.	III. EXHORTATION TO ENTER THE KINGDOM	239
	THE END OF THE WAY. *Hearers versus Doers.* Matthew 7:24-29.	
	APPENDIX	251

THE SERMON ON THE MOUNT

MATTHEW 5
(American Standard Version)

1 And seeing the multitudes, he went up into the mountain: and when he had sat down, his disciples came unto him: 2 and he opened his mouth and taught them, saying,

3 Blessed are the poor in spirit: for theirs is the kingdom of heaven.

4 Blessed are they that mourn: for they shall be comforted.

5 Blessed are the meek: for they shall inherit the earth.

6 Blessed are they that hunger and thirst after righteousness: for they shall be filled.

7 Blessed are the merciful: for they shall obtain mercy.

8 Blessed are the pure in heart: for they shall see God.

9 Blessed are the peacemakers: for they shall be called sons of God.

10 Blessed are they that have been persecuted for righteousness' sake: for theirs is the kingdom of heaven. 11 Blessed are ye when men shall reproach you, and persecute you, and say all manner of evil against you falsely, for my sake. 12 Rejoice, and be exceeding glad: for great is your reward in heaven: for so persecuted they the prophets that were before you.

13 Ye are the salt of the earth: but if the salt have lost its savor, wherewith shall it be salted? it is thenceforth good for nothing, but to be cast out and trodden under foot of men. 14 Ye are the light of the world. A city set on a hill cannot be hid. 15 Neither do men light a lamp, and put it under the bushel, but on the stand; and it shineth unto all that are in the house. 16 Even so let your light shine before men; that they may see your good works, and glorify your Father who is in heaven.

17 Think not that I came to destroy the law or the prophets: I came not to destroy, but to fulfil. 18 For verily I say unto you, Till heaven and earth pass away, one jot or one tittle shall in no wise pass away from the law, till all things be accomplished. 19 Whosoever therefore shall break one of these least commandments, and shall teach men so, shall be called least in the kingdom

of heaven: but whosoever shall do and teach them, he shall be called great in the kingdom of heaven. 20 For I say unto you, that except your righteousness shall exceed the righteousness of the scribes and Pharisees, ye shall in no wise enter into the kingdom of heaven.

21 Ye have heard that it was said to them of old time, Thou shalt not kill; and whosoever shall kill shall be in danger of the judgment: 22 but I say unto you, that every one who is angry with his brother shall be in danger of the judgment; and whosoever shall say to his brother, Raca, shall be in danger of the council; and whosoever shall say, Thou fool, shall be in danger of the hell of fire. 23 If therefore thou art offering thy gift at the altar, and there rememberest that thy brother hath aught against thee, 24 leave there thy gift. 25 Agree with thine adversary quickly, while thou art with him in the way; lest haply the adversary deliver thee to the judge, and the judge deliver thee to the officer, and thou be cast into prison. 26 Verily I say unto thee, Thou shalt by no means come out thence, till thou have paid the last farthing.

27 Ye have heard that it was said, Thou shalt not commit adultery: 28 but I say unto you, that every one that looketh on a woman to lust after her hath committed adultery with her already in his heart. 29 And if thy right eye causeth thee to stumble, pluck it out, and cast it from thee: for it is profitable for thee that one of thy members should perish, and not thy whole body be cast into hell. 30 And if thy right hand causeth thee to stumble, cut it off, and cast it from thee: for it is profitable for thee that one of thy members should perish, and not thy whole body go into hell. 31 It was said also, Whosoever shall put away his wife, let him give her a writing of divorcement: 32 but I say unto you, that every one that putteth away his wife, saving for the cause of fornication, maketh her an adulteress: and whosoever shall marry her when she is put away committeth adultery.

33 Again, ye have heard that it was said to them of old time, Thou shalt not forswear thyself, but shalt perform unto the Lord thine oaths: 34 but I say unto you, Swear not at all; neither by the heaven, for it is the throne of God; 35 nor by the earth, for it is the footstool of his feet; nor by Jerusalem, for it is the city of the great King. 36 Neither shalt thou swear by thy head, for thou canst not make one hair white or black. 37 But let your speech be, Yea, yea; Nay, nay: and whatsoever is more than these is of the evil one.

38 Ye have heard that it was said, An eye for an eye, and a tooth for a tooth: 39 but I say unto you, Resist not

him that is evil: but whosoever smiteth thee on thy right cheek, turn to him the other also. 40 And if any man would go to law with thee, and take away thy coat, let him have thy cloak also. 41 And whosoever shall compel thee to go one mile, go with him two. 42 Give to him that asketh thee, and from him that would borrow of thee turn not thou away.

43 Ye have heard that it was said, Thou shalt love thy neighbor, and hate thine enemy: 44 but I say unto you, Love your enemies, and pray for them that persecute you; 45 that ye may be sons of your Father who is in heaven: for he maketh his sun to rise on the evil and the good, and sendeth rain on the just and the unjust. 46 For if ye love them that love you, what reward have ye? do not even the publicans the same? 47 And if ye salute your brethren only, what do ye more than others? do not even the Gentiles the same? 48 Ye therefore shall be perfect, as your heavenly Father is perfect.

MATTHEW 6

(American Standard Version)

1 Take heed that ye do not your righteousness before men, to be seen of them: else ye have no reward with your Father who is in heaven.

2 When therefore thou doest alms, sound not a trumpet before thee, as the hypocrites do in the synagogues and in the streets, that they may have glory of men. Verily I say unto you, They have received their reward. 3 But when thou doest alms, let not thy left hand know what thy right hand doeth: 4 that thine alms may be in secret: and thy Father who seeth in secret shall recompense thee.

5 And when ye pray, ye shall not be as the hypocrites: for they love to stand and pray in the synagogues and in the corners of the streets, that they may be seen of men. Verily I say unto you, They have received their reward. 6 But thou, when thou prayest, enter into thine inner chamber, and having shut thy door, pray to thy Father who is in secret, and thy Father who seeth in secret shall recompense thee. 7 And in praying use not vain repetitions, as the Gentiles do: for they think that they shall be heard for their much speaking. 8 Be not therefore like unto them: for your Father knoweth what things ye have need of, before ye ask him. 9 After this manner therefore pray ye: Our Father who art in heaven, Hallowed be thy name. 10 Thy kingdom come. Thy will be done, as in heaven, so on earth. 11 Give us this day our

daily bread. 12 And forgive us our debts, as we also have forgiven our debtors. 13 And bring us not into temptation, but deliver us from the evil one. 14 For if ye forgive men their trespasses, your heavenly Father will also forgive you. 15 But if ye forgive not men their trespasses, neither will your Father forgive your trespasses.

16 Moreover when ye fast, be not, as the hypocrites, of a sad countenance: for they disfigure their faces, that they may be seen of men to fast. Verily I say unto you, They have received their reward. 17 But thou, when thou fastest, anoint thy head, and wash thy face; 18 that thou be not seen of men to fast, but of thy Father who is in secret: and thy Father, who seeth in secret, shall recompense thee.

19 Lay not up for yourselves treasures upon the earth, where moth and rust consume, and where thieves break through and steal: 20 but lay up for yourselves treasures in heaven, where neither moth nor rust doth consume, and where thieves do not break through nor steal: 21 for where thy treasure is, there will thy heart be also. 22 The lamp of the body is the eye: if therefore thine eye be single, thy whole body shall be full of light. 23 But if thine eye be evil, thy whole body shall be full of darkness. If therefore the light that is in thee be darkness, how great is the darkness! 24 No man can serve two masters: for either he will hate the one, and love the other; or else he will hold to one, and despise the other. Ye cannot serve God and mammon. 25 Therefore I say unto you, Be not anxious for your life, what ye shall eat, or what ye shall drink; nor yet for your body, what ye shall put on. Is not the life more than the food, and the body than the raiment? 26 Behold the birds of the heaven, that they sow not, neither do they reap, nor gather into barns; and your heavenly Father feedeth them. Are not ye of much more value than they? 27 And which of you by being anxious can add one cubit unto the measure of his life? 28 And why are ye anxious concerning raiment? Consider the lilies of the field, how they grow; they toil not, neither do they spin: 29 yet I say unto you, that even Solomon in all his glory was not arrayed like one of these. 30 But if God doth so clothe the grass of the field, which to-day is, and tomorrow is cast into the oven, shall he not much more clothe you, O ye of little faith? 31 Be not therefore anxious, saying, What shall we eat? or, What shall we drink? or, Wherewithal shall we be clothed? 32 For after all these things do the Gentiles seek; for your heavenly Father knoweth that ye have need of all these things. 33 But seek ye first his kingdom, and his righteousness; and all

these things shall be added unto you. 34 Be not therefore anxious for the morrow: for the morrow will be anxious for itself. Sufficient unto the day is the evil thereof.

MATTHEW 7
(American Standard Version)

1 Judge not, that ye be not judged. 2 For with what judgment ye judge, ye shall be judged: and with what measure ye mete, it shall be measured unto you. 3 And why beholdest thou the mote that is in thy brother's eye, but considerest not the beam that is in thine own eye? 4 Or how wilt thou say to thy brother, Let me cast out the mote out of thine eye; and lo, the beam is in thine own eye? 5 Thou hypocrite, cast out first the beam out of thine own eye; and then shalt thou see clearly to cast out the mote out of thy brother's eye.

6 Give not that which is holy unto the dogs, neither cast your pearls before the swine, lest haply they trample them under their feet, and turn and rend you.

7 Ask, and it shall be given you; seek, and ye shall find; knock, and it shall be opened unto you: 8 for every one that asketh receiveth; and he that seeketh findeth; and to him that knocketh it shall be opened. 9 Or what man is there of you, who, if his son shall ask him for a loaf, will give him a stone; 10 or if he shall ask for a fish, will give him a serpent? 11 If ye then, being evil, know how to give good gifts unto your children, how much more shall your Father who is in heaven give good things to them that ask him? 12 All things therefore whatsoever ye would that men should do unto you, even so do ye also unto them: for this is the law and the prophets.

13 Enter ye in by the narrow gate: for wide is the gate, and broad is the way, that leadeth to destruction, and many are they that enter in thereby. 14 For narrow is the gate, and straitened the way, that leadeth unto life, and few are they that find it.

15 Beware of false prophets, who come to you in sheep's clothing, but inwardly are ravening wolves. 16 By their fruits ye shall know them. Do men gather grapes of thorns, or figs of thistles? 17 Even so every good tree bringeth forth good fruit; but the corrupt tree bringeth forth evil fruit. 18 A good tree cannot bring forth evil fruit, neither can a corrupt tree bring forth good fruit. 19 Every tree that bringeth not forth good fruit is hewn down, and cast into the fire. 20 Therefore by

their fruits ye shall know them. 21 Not every one that saith unto me, Lord, Lord, shall enter into the kingdom of heaven; but he that doeth the will of my Father who is in heaven. 22 Many will say to me in that day, Lord, Lord, did we not prophesy by thy name, and by thy name cast out demons, and by thy name do many mighty works? 23 And then will I profess unto them, I never knew you: depart from me, ye that work iniquity.

24 Every one therefore that heareth these words of mine, and doeth them, shall be likened unto a wise man, who built his house upon the rock: 25 and the rain descended, and the floods came, and the winds blew, and beat upon that house; and it fell not: for it was founded upon the rock. 26 And every one that heareth these words of mine, and doeth them not, shall be likened unto a foolish man, who built his house upon the sand: 27 and the rain descended, and the floods came, and the winds blew, and smote upon that house; and it fell: and great was the fall thereof.

28 And it came to pass, when Jesus had finished these words, the multitudes were astonished at his teaching: 29 for he taught them as one having authority, and not as their scribes.

CHAPTER I

THE SERMON ON THE MOUNT

(INTRODUCTION)

MATTHEW 4:23—5:2.

"And Jesus went about in all Galilee, teaching in their synagogues, and preaching THE GOSPEL OF THE KINGDOM, and healing all manner of diseases and all manner of sickness among the people. And the report of him went forth into all Syria: and they brought unto him all that were sick, holden with divers diseases and torments, possessed with demons, and epileptic, and palsied; and he healed them. And there followed him great multitudes from Galilee and Decapolis and Jerusalem and Judea and from beyond Jordan. And seeing the multitudes, he went up into the mountain: and when he had sat down, his disciples came unto him: and he opened his mouth and taught them, saying....."

LUKE 6:11-13, 17-20b.

"But they were filled with madness; and communed one with another what they might do to Jesus. And it came to pass in these days, that he went out into the mountain to pray; and he continued all night in prayer to God. And when it was day, he called his disciples; and he chose from them twelve, whom he also named apostles . . . and he came down with them, and he stood on a level place, and a great multitude of his disciples, and a great number of the people from all Judea and Jerusalem and the seacoast of Tyre and Sidon, who came to hear him, and to be healed of their diseases; and they that were troubled with unclean spirits were healed. And all the multitude sought to touch him; for power came forth from him, and he healed them all. And he lifted up his eyes on his disciples, and said......"

Cf. also **MARK 3:13-15.**

I. FOR WHOM WAS THE SERMON ON THE MOUNT INTENDED?

At the very threshold of our discussion important questions arise. The question which constitutes the heading of this paragraph takes precedence over all others. There are those who claim that when Jesus delivered this sermon He neither directly or indirectly had in view the Church of today; that the precepts of this sermon are unlivable today, and were designed for another "dispensation." Why should we study a discourse which was not even intended for us?

There is, however, another view. Its contrast with the former is striking. According to it the Sermon on the Mount is for us the end of theology, the very essence of Christianity. Between these two extreme views there are many others. Enough has been said to indicate the importance of the aforementioned question.

A. IT WAS INTENDED FOR THE TWELVE AND FOR A LARGE GROUP OF OTHER DISCIPLES. Primarily for the disciples, Matt. 5:2, "..... his *disciples* came unto him: and he..... taught *them.*" Cf. Matt. 5:11, 14, 16, 48; Luke 6:20-23, 40. In all probability the Twelve formed a circle immediately around the Savior; farther down stood a large company of other disciples; beyond these, the multitude. Cf. Luke 6:17, 20; Matt. 5:1, 2.

B. IT WAS INTENDED FOR THE VAST MULTITUDE. Cf. Matt. 7:28, 29, "..... *the multitudes* were astonished at his teaching: for *he taught them* .....," also Luke 7:1.

C. Was It Also Intended for Us, for the Church of Today?

1. *The Dispensational View.* According to this view the Sermon on the Mount is not for our "dispensation." Says I. M. Haldeman, "The Sermon on the Mount must be taken in its wholeness and in its literalness. This sermon .....cannot be taken in its plain import and applied to Christians universally... It has been tried in spots, but....it has always been like planting a beautiful flower in stony ground or in a dry and withering atmosphere."[1] In the Scofield Bible we read, "For these reasons the Sermon on the Mount in its primary application gives neither the privilege nor the duty of the Church."[2]

Against this view we advance the following objections:

(*a*) It resembles modernism. Modernism rejects certain parts (or all) of Scripture as uninspired; the Dispensationalist regards several parts as "not meant for the Church." Result of either procedure, when consistently pursued: the nullification of Scripture as the ultimate standard of our thought and practice.

(*b*) It lacks proof. Jesus nowhere stated or indicated that the precepts contained in this sermon were intended for only one particular "dispensation." On the contrary, he emphasized the abiding character and validity of these precepts, Matt. 5:18.

(*c*) Cf. the objections against the theory of L. Tolstoy, which also hold against this view.

QUESTION FOR DISCUSSION. Just why is the dispensationalistic interpretation of this sermon *dangerous?*

2. *The View of L. Tolstoy, Russian novelist and social reformer.* His position: the Sermon on the Mount contains the essence of Christ's teaching which Christians should carry out entirely and literally. Christians should never participate in war; ground: Matt. 5:39, "Resist not evil." All oaths are wrong; ground: Matt. 5:34, "Swear not at all." Objections:

(*a*) The very thrust of the Sermon on the Mount is directed against the undiscriminating, two-dimension, crassly literal interpretation of the Pharisees, Cf. Matt. 5:21-48.

(*b*) Christ opposed this very error throughout his earthly sojourn. Cf. John 2:19; 3:3; 4:10, 32; 11:11; 14:4; Matt. 16:6, etc., etc.

(*c*) Christ himself did not carry out these precepts literally. Cf. Matt. 5:34; Matt. 26:63, 64.

(*d*) The very genius of the style and language employed (figurative) rules out this view.

(*e*) The various admonitions contained in this sermon should be read and interpreted in the light of their specific context. When this is done, it will become apparent that Tolstoy's view is untenable.

3. *The Prevailing Modernistic View.* Briefly stated it is as follows, "We do not believe in theology; we believe in the Sermon on the Mount. It contains all we need to know in order to live as Christians. It contains no blood-theology; only ethics, no doctrine." Objections:

(*a*) Modernists proceed very arbitrarily when they *accept* the Sermon on the Mount and *reject* those sayings of Jesus in which he (1) demands faith in himself as present Savior and future Judge, Matt. 16:15; 22:42; John 14:1;[3] (2) clearly teaches the doctrine of the Atonement by blood, Matt. 20:28; Mk. 10:45; John 3:14-17 (cf. John 1:29).

(*b*) The reason why the doctrine of the Atonement by blood is not *emphasized* in this sermon is that in God's wisdom the *facts* of redemption precede the *doctrines* of redemption.[4] The full import of the significance of Christ's death is not yet pointed out in this sermon for the simple reason that Christ had not yet died. Cf. also John 16:12 ff.

4. *The Only Tenable View.* Inasmuch as Christ in this beautiful discourse deals with the fundamental principles of conduct which according to his own testimony remain the same in every age, Matt. 5:17, 18, it follows that this sermon was intended for Christ's disciples living today as well as for those who surrounded him when he delivered it. Christ thought of us even in his prayers, John 17:20, 21.

SUBJECT FOR DISCUSSION. Mention a few very practical subjects treated in this sermon. Cf. Matt. 5:21, 27, 33, 38; 6:1, 5, 16, 19, 25; 7:1, 6, 7, 12, 24. Cf. P. Mauro, *The Gospel of the Kingdom,* Chap. XI.

II. WHAT IS THE HISTORICAL BACKGROUND OF THIS SERMON?

A. THE CONTROVERSY WITH THE PHARISEES.

In all probability Jesus preached this sermon during the second year of his ministry, in the

Spring of the year, in the early hours of the morning. Cf. John 2:13; 5:1; Luke 6:1, 12, 13, 20. The main previous events in Christ's ministry: baptism, temptation, first miracle at Cana, early Judæan ministry, return to Galilee through Samaria, early miracles in and around Capernaum, and return to Jerusalem for the second Passover. Then follow three Sabbath controversies between Christ and the Pharisees, John 5; Lk. 6:1-15; Lk. 6:6-11. As a result of these healings on the Sabbath the Pharisees flare up in anger, John 5:18; Lk. 6:11. Yet the *real* point at issue was not the Sabbath question as such, but the underlying contrast between Christ's deeply spiritual interpretation of the Law and the literal interpretation of the Pharisees. Hence, in the Sermon on the Mount Christ gives us the true, spiritual meaning of the Law and over against the accusations of the Pharisees exhibits himself as the Fulfiller of the Law. Cf. Matt. 5:17-48.

B. THE PRAYER.

Notice the wonderful contrast indicated in Lk. 6:11, 12, "But *they* were filled with *madness* ..... *he* went out into the mountain to *pray.*" Consider that the Sermon on the Mount was preached the morning after Christ spent a whole night in prayer, and it will add much to your appreciation of the discourse.

QUESTION FOR DISCUSSION. Christ prayed before he delivered the sermon. Was this really necessary for Christ? (Hint: *a.* remember Christ's two natures; *b.* what is prayer?). What lessons for our own life can we derive from this prayer of Christ?

C. The Choosing of the Disciples.

The prayer is followed by the choosing of the disciples, Lk. 6:13. How appropriate that after the appointment of the apostles as preachers of the Gospel of the Kingdom Christ in this sermon "teaches" (Matt. 5:2) them this Gospel!

D. The Healing of the Sick.

The choosing of the Twelve is followed by the healing of many sick. Cf. Matt. 4:23, 24; Luke 6:18, 19. Then follows the sermon. How fitting that Christ, having shown himself to be the Great Physician for the body, now by means of this discourse reveals himself as also the Great Physician for the soul! Cf. Heb. 7:25.

III. WHERE WAS THIS SERMON DELIVERED?

A. In Galilee, Matt. 4:23.

That the place is not without significance is plain from Matt. 4:12-17. For the scene of this sermon Jesus chose the "region of the shadow of death!"

B. On the Mountain Near Capernaum, Matt. 5:1; 8:5; Lk. 7:1.

1. *Apparent contrast between Matthew and Luke.* Luke says, "....on a level place," Lk. 6:17. Matthew, "on the mountain." The seeming contradiction disappears either by supposing that Christ preached the sermon on a mountain-plain; or, that having chosen his disciples on the mountain-top, he with them descended to a plain where he healed the sick, and afterward with the disciples returned to the top. We

prefer the latter interpretation (1) in view of Mk. 3:13; Lk. 6:17; Matt. 5:1; and (2) because it also explains why Luke can speak of Christ as "standing" while Matthew pictures him as "sitting." In the plain he "stood" to heal the sick; on the mountain-top he "sat," according to oriental custom, Mk. 4:1; 9:35; 13:3; Lk. 4:20, to deliver the sermon.

2. *Importance of the place.* The Authorized Version has "*a* mountain"; the American Standard Version has "*the* mountain." The latter is correct. In all probability the definite article ("the") points *not* to the mountain-district in general but to a well-known mountain near Capernaum. Tradition points to the *Horns of Hattin,* named thus because these peaks resemble two horns when seen from afar—about four miles back from the Sea of Galilee and about eight miles southwest of Capernaum. Certainty is lacking.

What a difference between this mountain and Horeb! Horeb: cold, bleak, barren, inaccessible; a howling wilderness, fiery serpents, poisonous basilisks. Here: a smiling landscape, shrubs and trees, the green grass of the heights with daisies, anemones, and hyacinths blooming here and there. At Horeb God appearing in thunder and lightning, and the people overcome with fear. Here: the Son of Man, the Immanuel, grace and truth proceeding from his lips, sitting down in the midst of his disciples who listen without fear or trembling. Yet we must be careful. Horeb and the Mount of the Beatitudes complement each other. The Law proclaimed on Horeb is not set aside, but is given its true deeply spiritual interpretation on the Mount of the Beatitudes.

REFERENCES

1) I. M. HALDEMAN, *The Kingdom of God*, p. 149. Cf. P. MAURO, *The Gospel of the Kingdom*.
2) p. 1000.
3) W. FAIRWEATHER, *The Background of the Gospels*, p. 309.
4) T. D. BERNARD, *The Progress of Doctrine*, p. 34; G. VOS, *Concerning the Kingdom of God and the Church*, p. 116.

READING AND STUDY HELPS

1. For a bibliography on The Sermon, see A. Tholuck, *Commentary on the Sermon on the Mount*, pp. 41-49; also A. T. Robertson, *Syllabus*, pp. 152-154.

2. Consult commentaries on Matthew and on Luke, e. g., L. Abbott, W. C. Allen in the *I. C. C.*, Alexander, C. J. Ellicott, J. M. Gibson in *The Expositor's Bible*, vol. IV, J. P. Lange, R. C. H. Lenski, H. A. W. Meyer, G. C. Morgan, Matthew Henry, A. T. Robertson, etc. Dutch: Grosheide, Matthew Henry, J. Van Andel (Lukas).

3. Special works on the Sermon on the Mount. The literature is enormous. We shall mention only a few works: Augustine, *The Sermon on the Mount, with Observations by R. C. Trench;* J. O. Dykes, *The Beatitudes, Laws, Relations of the Kingdom* (3 vols.); D. A. Hayes, *The Heights of Christian Living;* M. Loy, *The Sermon on the Mount;* E. Lyttleton, *Studies in the Sermon on the Mount;* C. B. McAfee, *Studies in the Sermon on the Mount;* R. B. Miller, art. *Sermon on the Mount* in *I. S. B. E.;* A. Tholuck, *Commentary on the Sermon on the Mount;* C. C. Chappell, *The Sermon on the Mount.* Dutch: L. S. Jongsma, *De Bergrede*, etc.

4. For the geographical setting see esp. the *Bible Atlas* by J. L. Hurlbut and J. H. Vincent.

CHAPTER II

THEME AND OUTLINE OF THE SERMON ON THE MOUNT

> MATTHEW 4:23—"And Jesus went about in all Galilee..... preaching THE GOSPEL OF THE KINGDOM......"
>
> MATTHEW 5:3—"Blessed are the poor in spirit, for theirs is THE KINGDOM OF HEAVEN." Cf. Luke 6:20.
>
> MATTHEW 5:10—"Blessed are they that have been persecuted for righteousness' sake: for theirs is THE KINGDOM OF HEAVEN."
>
> MATTHEW 5:19, 20—"Whosoever therefore shall break one of these least commandments and shall teach men so, shall be called least in THE KINGDOM OF HEAVEN: but whosoever shall do and teach them, he shall be called great in THE KINGDOM OF HEAVEN. For I say unto you, that except your righteousness shall exceed the righteousness of the scribes and Pharisees, ye shall in no wise enter into THE KINGDOM OF HEAVEN."
>
> MATTHEW 6:10—"THY KINGDOM come. Thy will be done as in heaven, so on earth."
>
> MATTHEW 6:13b in A. V.—"For thine is THE KINGDOM, and the power and the glory, forever. Amen."
>
> MATTHEW 6:33—"But seek ye first HIS KINGDOM......"
>
> MATTHEW 7:21—"Not every one.... shall enter into THE KINGDOM OF HEAVEN......"

I. THE THEME OF THIS SERMON.

A. PRESUPPOSITION: THE SERMON (Matt. 5-7) IS A COHERENT WHOLE.

1. *View of Higher Criticism Tested.* According to the prevailing teaching of Higher Criticism Matthew 5-7 does not contain one continued

and connected discourse, but rather a group of sayings spoken at different times and united by Matthew *as if* delivered at one time. For us who believe in the inspiration of Scripture it is impossible to subscribe to this view, for Matthew and Luke clearly intend to convey the impression that all these sayings were spoken at one time and constitute one single sermon. The entire discourse is preceded by these words, "And he opened his mouth and taught them saying...." It is followed by: "And it came to pass when Jesus had finished these words...." Cf. Luke 6:20 and Luke 7:1.

2. *Matthew and Luke Give Different Accounts of the SAME Sermon.* Grounds:

(*a*) The historical setting is the same in both Gospels: in both it is preceded by the account of a great multitude flocking to Jesus to be healed and followed by the story of the healing of the centurion's servant. Cf. Matt. 5:1 with Luke 6:17; Matt. 4:23 with Luke 6:17-19; Matt. 8:5 with Luke 7:2.

(*b*) The train of thought is the same in both: the Beatitudes, the supremacy of the law of love, the parable of the two builders. Cf. Matt. 5:3-12 with Luke 6:20-23; Matt. 5:43-48 with Luke 6:27-38; Matt. 7:24-27 with Luke 6:47-49.

(*c*) The difference is due to the fact that Matthew and Luke had different readers in mind. Matthew, who *primarily* had in mind the Jews, includes more material which has direct reference to the Pharisaic misinterpretation of the Law. Cf. Matt. 5:17 - 6:18.

B. Theme: The Gospel of the Kingdom.

1. *Proof:*

(*a*) The Sermon is introduced as The Gospel of the Kingdom, Matt. 4:23. This introduces not merely *this* sermon, but in a sense *all* the discourses of Jesus, cf. his parables (Matt. 13).

(*b*) The expression, "the kingdom of heaven," occurs again and again. See the passages quoted at the head of this chapter.

2. *Meaning of the Term "Kingdom of Heaven, or Kingdom of God."* Dr. G. Vos has called this theme, "the most profoundly *religious* of all biblical conceptions."[1]

(*a*) It does not refer to an earthly, temporal, exclusively material, Jewish kingdom. According to Premillennialists Jesus came on earth in order to establish a political kingdom, covenanted to the Jews. He announced this kingdom as "at hand," i. e., about to be established, but the Jews did not want it: they "morally rejected" it; hence, it is now postponed to another "dispensation."[2] That this theory is erroneous is very evident when one examines such passages as Matt. 5:3, "Blessed are the poor .... for theirs IS the kingdom of heaven." Cf. Matt. 5:10; 6:10; 12:28; 19:14; Mk. 12:34; Lk. 17:20, 21; John 3:3; 18:36; Rom. 14:17, etc., etc.

(*b*) It does not refer to two kingdoms: one, the kingdom of heaven; the other, the kingdom of God. The Scofield Bible tells us that the kingdom of heaven is to be distinguished from the kingdom of God in five respects. Its index speaks of the two kingdoms "contrasted."[3]

However, even some eminent Pre's have discarded this altogether untenable view. So, e. g., Rev. W. B. Riley, "I do not think there is any difference .... the phraseology in the New Testament uses the terms interchangeably."[4] The fact that the two terms have reference to one and the same kingdom is evident from a comparison between Matt. 4:17 and Mk. 1:14; Matt. 11:11 and Lk. 7:28; Matt. 5:3 and Lk. 6:20; Matt. 13:31 and Mk. 4:30, 31; Matt. 19:14 and Mk. 10:14; Matt. 19:23, 24, and Mk. 10:23, 24.

QUESTION FOR DISCUSSION. How is it that Matthew uses the term "Kingdom of Heaven"; Luke, "Kingdom of God"?

(c) The term "kingdom of heaven or of God" indicates *GOD'S KINGSHIP, REIGN or SOVEREIGNTY, recognized in the hearts and operative in the lives of his people, and effecting their COMPLETE SALVATION, their constitution as a CHURCH, and catastrophically a REDEEMED UNIVERSE*. Notice especially the four concepts:

(1) God's kingship, reign, or recognized sovereignty. That may be the meaning in Lk. 17:21, "The kingdom of God is within you," and *is* the meaning in Matt. 6:10, "Thy kingdom come, thy *will* be done ......"

(2) Complete salvation, i. e., all the spiritual blessings which result when God is King in our hearts, recognized and obeyed as such. That is the meaning, according to the context, in Mk. 10:25, 26, "It is easier .... than for a rich man to enter *the kingdom of God*. And they ... said, *"Then who can be saved?"*

(3) The church: the community of men in whose hearts God is recognized as King. Kingdom of God and church when used in this sense are *nearly* equivalent. This is the meaning in Matt. 16:18, 19, ".... and upon this rock will I build my *church*..... I will give unto thee the keys of the *kingdom of heaven*."

QUESTION FOR DISCUSSION. What is the difference between the Kingdom of God and the Church?

(4) The redeemed universe: the new heaven and earth with all their glory; something still *future*: the final realization of God's saving power. Thus in Matt. 25:34, "..... inherit *the kingdom prepared for you*......"

(*d*) These four meanings are not separate and unrelated. They all proceed from the central idea of the reign of God, his supremacy in the sphere of saving power. The kingdom (or kingship: the Greek word has both meanings) of heaven is like a gradually developing mustard seed; hence, both present and future. It is present; study Matt. 5:3, 10; 12:28; 13:11, 19, 24, 31, 52; 19:14; Mk. 9:1; 10:15; 12:34; Lk. 7:28; 17:20, 21; John 3:3-5; 18:36; Rom. 14:17; I Cor. 4:20; 15:24, 25; Col. 1:13; 4:11. It is future; study Matt. 7:21, 22; 25:34; 26:29; I Cor. 6:9; 15:50; Gal. 5:21; Eph. 5:5; I Thess. 2:12; II Thess. 1:5, etc.

(*e*) Jesus spoke of the work of salvation as the kingdom or reign of *heaven* in order to indicate the *supernatural* character, origin, and purpose of our salvation. Our salvation begins in heaven and should redound to the glory of the

Father in heaven. Hence, by using this term Christ defended the truth, so precious to all Calvinists, that everything is subservient to God's glory.

QUESTION FOR DISCUSSION. Why did Jesus stress the heavenly, supernatural nature of salvation? Should this be stressed today? What is the Ritschlian conception of the Kingdom?

II. OUTLINE OF THE SERMON ON THE MOUNT (Be sure to trace this in your Bible and to become thoroughly familiar with it):

THE GOSPEL OF THE KINGDOM OF HEAVEN
(Introductory verse: Matt. 5:1)

I. THE CITIZENS OF THE KINGDOM, Matt. 5:2-16.
  A. Their character and blessedness, vss. 2-12 (The Beatitudes)
  B. Their relation to the world, vss. 13-16:
    1) They are the *salt* of the earth, vs. 13;
    2) They are the *light* of the world, vss. 14-16.

II. THE RIGHTEOUSNESS OF THE KINGDOM, Matt. 5:17-7:12.
  A. This righteousness is in full accord with the moral law of the O. T., vss. 17-19.
    1) It does not destroy but it fulfills the law, vss. 17, 18.
    2) Accordingly, reward is promised to those who keep the Law, and punishment is threatened upon those who disobey it, vs. 19.
  B. This righteousness is *not* in conformity with the current and traditional Jewish *interpretation* and *application* of the Law, vss. 20-48;

1) It exceeds the righteousness (conformity to the Law) of the scribes and Pharisees of Jesus' day, vs. 20.
2) It also exceeds the righteousness of ancient Jewish interpreters, vss. 21-48.

   This contrast pointed out with respect to the interpretation of:
   a. the sixth commandment, vss. 21-26,
   b. the seventh commandment, vss. 27-32,
   c. the third commandment, vss. 33-37,
   d. the law of retaliation, vss. 38-42,
   e. the fundamental law of love, vss. 33-48.

C. The essence of this righteousness with respect to our relation to *God*: *"love God above all!"*

   It consists in *secret devotion to* and *unlimited trust in* God, Matt. 6.
   1) The secret devotion of the heart rather than the merely outward deed "to be seen of men," vss. 1-18. This principle illustrated with respect to:
      a. alms-giving, vss. 1-4.
      b. prayer, vss. 5-15.
      c. fasting, vss. 16-18.
   2) Unlimited trust in God rather than an attempt to worship both God and mammon, vss. 19-34:
      a. This trust is incompatible with mammon-worship, vss. 19-24.

       b. It is also incompatible with worry, vss. 25-32.

       c. It is based on the assurance that to those who seek the Kingdom of God .... all things shall be added, vss. 33, 34.

  D. The essence of this righteousness with respect to our relation to *man*: *"love thy neighbor as thyself":*

     It consists in *absence of censoriousness, discrimination in judgment,* i. e., in *the application of the Golden Rule,* Matt. 7:1-13.

    1) Absence of censoriousness, vss. 1-5.
    2) Discrimination in judgment, vs. 6.
    3) Wisdom to judge aright obtained by prayer, vss. 7-11.
    4) The Golden Rule, vs. 12.

III. EXHORTATION TO ENTER THE KINGDOM, Matt. 7:13-27.

  A. The Beginning of the way, vss. 13, 14.
  B. Progress upon the way, vss. 15-20.
  C. The end of the way: sayers versus doers, vss. 21-23.
  D. The end of the way: hearers versus doers, vss. 24-27.

     Concluding verses: the impression of the sermon on the hearers, vss. 28, 29.

REFERENCES

[1] G. VOS, *Concerning the Kingdom of God and the Church,* p. 192.

[2] I. M. HALDEMAN, *The Kingdom of God,* pp. 169-171, 188, 189, ff.; *Scofield Bible,* p. 1011; *Report of the Proph.*

Conf. of 1914, p. 160; C. LARKIN, *Second Coming*, p. 47; *Grace and Glory*, April 1931; H. BULTEMA, *Maranatha*, pp. 273, 274.

3) p. 1003.

4) W. B. RILEY, *Light on Prophecy*, p. 343.

READING AND STUDY HELPS

1. For the relation between Matthew's and Luke's account see *I. S. B. E.* articles on *The Sermon on the Mount and Sermon on the Plain.*

2. For the unity of the sermon see Grosheide, op. cit., p. 96 ff.; Tholuck, op. cit., pp. 1-7.

3. For the meaning of the term "Kingdom of Heaven" see G. Vos, *The Kingdom of God and the Church;* Stalker, art. in *I. S. B. E.* and *The Ethics of Jesus*, p. 51 ff.; H. Bavinck, *Gereformeerde Dogmatiek*, III, 256 ff., 561 ff.; IV., 322, 737; P. Mauro, *The Gospel of the Kingdom;* A. Kuyper, Jr., *Van Het Koninkrijk der Hemelen;* L. Berkhof, *Het Koninkrijk Gods*, articles which appeared in *De Wachter* Feb. 5, 1919, to Sept. 1, 1920; and A. Robertson, *Regnum Dei.*

4. For the train of thought see esp. Tholuck, op. cit., pp. 13-17; A. B. Bruce, *The Training of the Twelve*, page 42 ff.

5. For a convenient outline to compare with my own, see P. Vollmer, *Modern Students' Life of Christ*, pp. 118, 119.

6. The liberal view is given, e. g., by W. Rauschenbusch in his *Theology for the Social Gospel.*

CHAPTER III

THE CITIZENS OF THE KINGDOM: THEIR CHARACTER AND BLESSEDNESS
(THE BEATITUDES)

MATTHEW 5:3-5.
"Blessed are the poor in spirit: for theirs is the kingdom of heaven. Blessed are they that mourn: for they shall be comforted. Blessed are the meek: for they shall inherit the earth."

Cf. **LUKE 6:20, 21.**
"Blessed are ye poor: for yours is the kingdom of God.....Blessed are ye that weep now: for ye shall laugh."

I. THE BEATITUDES CONSIDERED AS A GROUP.

A. EACH BEATITUDE CONSISTS OF THREE PARTS: (1) an Ascription of Blessedness ("Blessed"); (2) a Description of Character ("the poor in spirit".... "the meek"); and (3) a Promise or Description of Blessedness ("theirs is the Kingdom of heaven").

1. *The Ascription of Blessedness.* Every beatitude begins with the word "Blessed." The original word is *makarios*, pl. *makarioi*. This word does not refer to those who are considered happy by *others*, nor in the first place to those who consider *themselves* happy, but it refers to those who *are* blessed whether they are *considered* such or not. Surely, the poor and those persecuted are not *considered* happy; surely, they that mourn are not expressing their joy!

For both of these ideas the Greek uses other words. The blessedness here spoken of is a matter not of feeling, but of inner spiritual condition or state; the Christian possesses this felicity whether he is at all times conscious of it or not. The Aramaic word which Christ probably used is similar to the Hebrew word which is found in Ps. 31:1, *"Blessed* is he whose transgression is forgiven." Cf. Psalms 1:1; 2:12; 32:2; 33:12; 34:8; 40:4; 41:4, etc. It means *"superlatively blessed, most blessed"* (Dutch: welgelukzalig). It pertains only to those in whose hearts God has begun the work of saving grace. Cf. Ps. 32:1; Rom. 4:7, 8; Rev. 14:13; 20:6.

2. *The Description of Character.* When Jesus speaks about "the poor," "the meek," etc., he does not refer to eight different classes of people: some mourners, others meek, etc., but to one class only. These eight sentences describe the character of the citizen of the Kingdom in its psychological development.

3. *The Description of Blessedness.* There is a definite relation between the character indicated and the blessing described. This relation is one of *contrast* in the first three and in the eighth beatitude: the *poor* are said to *possess a kingdom;* the *meek* are said to *inherit the earth.* It is a relation of *correspondence* in the fourth, fifth, sixth, and seventh beatitudes: the *hungry* will be *filled;* the *merciful* will obtain *mercy,* etc.

The description of blessedness is at the same

time a description of the Kingdom of Heaven. The first and the last beatitudes mention the kingdom of heaven, Matt. 5:3, 10; the intervening beatitudes describe the nature of that kingdom. The Jews expected a physical, political, Jewish kingdom. In these beatitudes Jesus, on the contrary, pictures to them the Kingdom of heaven as consisting of comfort or spiritual joy (second beatitude), inheritance (third beatitude), a full measure of righteousness (fourth beatitude), mercy or pardon (fifth beatitude), the vision of God (sixth beatitude), and adoption and recognition as sons (seventh beatitude). Cf. the description of the Kingdom of heaven in Rom. 14:17. Hence, the term "kingdom of heaven," as used in the beatitudes, refers to the blessings enjoyed by those in whose hearts God is acknowledged as King, i. e., it refers to complete salvation. Cf. Outline II, I, B, 2, c.

QUESTION FOR DISCUSSION. Can you suggest any reason why Jesus begins his Sermon on the Mount with beatitudes?

B. THESE BEATITUDES REVEAL A BEAUTIFUL ORDER OF ARRANGEMENT.

They reveal successively the *beginning, progress,* and *perfection of the faith of the citizens of the Kingdom,* and the *persecution to which this faith is subjected*:

1. *The Beginning of Faith.* The first experience of a person who turns from darkness to light is knowledge of misery, a consciousness of his spiritual poverty; hence, the first beatitude is, "Blessed are the poor in spirit....." Next,

this person will search for the reason of his spiritual poverty, namely, his own guilt over which he then begins to mourn. Hence, the second beatitude, "Blessed are they that mourn ..." This consciousness of guilt humiliates him. Hence, the third beatitude, "Blessed are the meek or humble-minded." These three beatitudes may be called negative beatitudes; beatitudes of conscious want or poverty.

2. *The Progress of Faith.* Conscious of his own poverty and lack, the sinner begins to hunger for a righteousness not his own. Hence, the fourth beatitude, "Blessed are they that hunger and thirst after righteousness...." The beatitude of conscious desire.

3. *The Perfection of Faith.* The soul that hungers and thirsts after righteousness receives righteousness, i. e., he receives mercy, purity of heart, and a peace which makes peace. Hence, beatitudes five, six, and seven. Cf. Matt. 5:7-9.

4. *The Persecution to Which Faith is Subjected.* This is expressed in the eighth beatitude, Matt. 5:10-12.

These eight features of Christian character develop successively. Yet, as the flower-bud already contains the flower, so the earliest grace (consciousness of "spiritual poverty") already contains all the others in its bosom, and is itself never lost.

C. Nearly All of These Beatitudes Are Paradoxical in Character.

This fact should be emphasized. It is very important. The dictionary defines a paradox as "an expression seemingly though not necessarily absurd or self-contradictory in its terms." The Bible is replete with paradoxes. The reason for this is the fact that it reveals to us a salvation which is "from above," which is "unto the Gentiles *foolishness.*" It teaches us "the things of the Spirit" which are "foolishness" unto natural man; he cannot know them for they are "spiritually judged." Scripture introduces us to the world of eternity. That world of eternity is so different from our own that it is impossible for the mind of natural man to understand its mysteries. Even the regenerated individual needs the constant guidance of the Holy Spirit in order to "see" the kingdom of God. Man can never "figure out" the way of salvation. It must be "revealed" to him. No wonder, therefore, that Scripture is full of "paradoxes." Notice the following which occur in the N. T.:

"Blessed are the *poor . . . they that mourn . . . . the meek . . . . . they that hunger and thirst . . . . . they that have been persecuted."* Matt. 5:3-10.

"Blessed are ye when men shall reproach you, and persecute you, and say all manner of evil against you falsely for my sake. Rejoice, and be exceeding glad: for great is your reward in heaven. . . . ." Matt. 5:11, 12. In amazement we ask, "How *can* these things be true?"

The paradoxical nature of these utterances is even more striking when one considers that according to the original the meaning is about as follows, note the italics: "Blessed they that are mourning, for *just they* (or: *they alone*) shall be comforted. Blessed the meek, for *just they* (or: *they alone*) shall inherit the earth."

"*Ye alone* are the salt of the earth. *Ye alone* are the light of the world." Matt. 5:13, 14.

"*Keep on* loving your *enemies, continue to pray for them who continue to persecute you.*" Matt. 5:44.

"For whosoever would *save* his life shall *lose* it; but whosoever shall *lose* his life for my sake, the same shall *save* it." Lk. 9:24.

"..... it was God's good pleasure through the *foolishness* of the preaching to *save* them that believe .... Because the *foolishness of God* (!) is *wiser* than men; and the *weakness of God* (!) is *stronger* than men." I Cor. 1:20-25.

".... in everything *commending* ourselves ... as *deceivers and yet true; as unknown and yet well-known; as dying and behold we live; as chastened and not killed; as sorrowful, yet always rejoicing; as poor, yet making many rich; as having nothing, and yet possessing all things.*" II Cor. 6:4-10.

"*Wherefore I take pleasure in weaknesses, in injuries, in necessities, in persecutions, in distresses, for Christ's sake: for WHEN I AM WEAK, THEN AM I STRONG!*" II Cor. 12:10.

".... and to *know* the love of Christ which *passeth knowledge.*" Eph. 3:19.

"By faith he (Moses) forsook Egypt, not fearing the wrath of the king: for he endured, as *seeing* him who is *invisible.*" Heb. 11:27.

It is well for us to stress this thought. The truth contained in Scripture is not a product of the human mind. It is far above us. It is a *revelation*. Even the regenerate cannot *fully* understand it, for it is *divine*. The doctrine of salvation *is* not absurd, to be sure. Our worship of God which answers to his revelation is, indeed, a LOGIKE LATREIA, a *rational* (not: rationalistic) *worship;* but to the mind of natural man these things do not *seem* rational but foolish and absurd. Moreover, even the believer humbly accepts the divine declaration, "For *my* thoughts are not *your* thoughts, neither are *your* ways *my* ways, saith Jehovah. For as the heavens are higher than the earth, so are *my* ways higher than *your* ways, and *my* thoughts than *your* thoughts." Is. 55:8, 9. Though we indeed use our reasoning powers whenever we reflect upon God's revelation, yet God and his way of salvation remain *incomprehensible*. Job 11:7, "Canst thou by searching find out God? Canst thou find out the Almighty unto perfection? It is high as heaven; what canst thou do? Deeper than Sheol; what canst thou know?" Job 26:14, "Lo, these are but the outskirts of his ways: And how small a whisper do we hear of him! But the thunder of his power who can understand?" Is. 40:28, "..... there is no searching of his understanding."

Accordingly, the paradox does not only characterize certain specific expressions or passages of Scripture but the whole of Scripture from beginning to end. We cannot *fully understand* how a universe could be created out of *nothing;* how man, created in God's image and after his likeness, could *fall;* how Christ can be at one and the same time *God and man, infinite* in knowledge, power, etc., and yet *finite;* how God can declare the *sinner . . . . . just;* how the *just* (Christ) *can ever* take the place of and suffer for the *unjust;* how the *righteousness* of Christ can ever by all the laws of logic be *imputed* to us; and how it is ever possible that "the *dead* shall *hear* the voice of the Son of God, and they that hear shall live." We gladly accept these mysteries. We confess, however, that although the mind of the regenerated man when illumined by the Holy Spirit *can* and *should approach* them, it can never *comprehend* them. If it could *comprehend* them, i. e., understand them *fully*, they would cease to be *divine.* Hence, they would cease to be believable. Now we accept and believe them.

In these beatitudes this *other*ness of the laws which pertain to the kingdom of heaven is beautifully revealed to us. *"Oh the blessedness of . . . . the poor, the mourners, the meek, the hungry, the persecuted! They, they alone are blessed."*

QUESTIONS FOR DISCUSSION. What seems to be the outstanding characteristic of Barthianism, a religious movement with which we should all be acquainted? How does our view differ from Barth's teaching with reference to the *paradox?*

II. THE BEGINNING OF FAITH: THE FIRST THREE BEATITUDES.

A. THE FIRST BEATITUDE.

1. *"Blessed are the poor in spirit . . . ."*

(*a*) The world says just the opposite, "Blessed

are the rich," etc. Jesus says, "Blessed are the poor, mourners, meek, hungry," etc. Reason: one's *outward condition* may be ever so enviable; in the end it vanishes like a dream. God never made a soul so small that the whole world will satisfy it. The *inner state and character of the soul* abides. Cf. Luke 12:15; I Cor. 7:31.

(*b*) "The poor in spirit." The New Testament uses two words for "poor." The one refers to a pauper, one so poor that he must daily work for his bread. The other word, the one used here, is even stronger: it indicates not the pauper but the beggar, the one who lives not by his own labor but on other men's alms. Cf. Luke 16:20, 21. While the pauper has nothing superfluous, the beggar has nothing at all.[1] The cringingly poor individual is meant, the one who is conscious of the fact that he is completely helpless in himself, and is also completely dependent upon the mercy of God. Consequently, the "poor *in spirit*" are those who recognize their spiritual poverty: who recognize that they have *nothing*. Poverty of spirit contains two elements: *a*) consciousness of misery and want; *b*) brokenness of old pride, so that one cries out, "God, be merciful to me, a sinner." This poverty is inwrought by the Holy Spirit, John 3:5. Jesus here paves the way for the Pauline doctrine of salvation by grace, justification through faith in Christ's merits.

QUESTION FOR DISCUSSION. Luke has, "Blessed are ye poor." Matthew has, "Blessed are the poor *in spirit*." Is there a providential relation between material poverty and the recognition of spiritual poverty?

2. ". . . . . *for theirs is the kingdom of heaven.*"

(*a*) For the meaning of the term "kingdom of heaven" see this Outline, I, A, 3, and Outline II, I, B, 2.

(*b*) Grammar permits two constructions: (1) The kingdom of heaven *consists* of the poor in spirit; (2) it *belongs* to the poor in spirit. The second meaning is correct inasmuch as kingdom of heaven means salvation here: pardon, adoption, etc., Eph. 1:3. Though they are poor, yet they are rich!

B. THE SECOND BEATITUDE.

1. "*Blessed are they that mourn.*"

(*a*) Relation to first beatitude. This is illustrated in the Parable of the Prodigal Son. First he sees his poverty and says, "I perish here with hunger," cf. first beatitude. Then he begins to see his sin as the cause of his misery, "Father, I have *sinned* . . . ." Cf. Luke 15:17-19. In view of the context not all mourners are called blessed, but only those who mourn because of their spiritual poverty. Cf. II Cor. 7:10. It is a sorrow because of sin, not merely because of the consequence of sin.

(*b*) ". . . . they that mourn." The original word for mourning indicates a sorrow which begins in the heart, takes possession of the whole person, and is outwardly manifested.[2]

2. "*. . . for they shall be comforted.*"

(*a*) Godly sorrow causes the soul to seek God's mercy. God, in turn, grants comfort to those who come unto him with their burden of sin desiring forgiveness and wishing to live a new and holy life. God himself caused them to come. Thus, tears like raindrops, fall to the ground and come up in flowers. Cf. Eccl. 7:2, 3; Is. 61:2, 3, etc. This passage does *not* teach that the mourners will be comforted during an earthly millennium. Though some interpret it thus, this interpretation is entirely foreign to the context.

(*b*) The original term for "comforted" contains the word *Paraclete,* John 14:16, 26; 15:26; 16:7; I John 2:1. The word has a very broad meaning, much broader than our English word "comfort." It means to call a person to one's side in order to help him in any way, e. g., by pleading his cause or by admonishing him or by instructing him or by imparting consolation to him. Cf. I Cor. 14:3; Rom. 12:8. The mourner will receive a Paraclete, i. e., a Helper, hence an Advocate, Intercessor, Comforter.[3] Both Christ and the Holy Spirit will plead his cause and help him.

QUESTION FOR DISCUSSION. Jesus says, "Blessed are they that mourn." Should not Christians be optimists?

C. THE THIRD BEATITUDE.

1. *"Blessed are the meek . . . . . ."*

(*a*) Relation to first and second beatitudes. The prodigal son first sees his poverty, "I perish here with hunger," cf. first beatitude; then he sees the cause of his poverty, "Father, I have *sinned,*" (cf. second beatitude); as a result he becomes aware of his own unworthiness, "I am no more worthy to be called thy son," i. e., he becomes meek. Cf. Luke 15:17-19.

(*b*) Meekness means that humility of spirit which results from the death of self-righteousness and from confession of sin. It refers to a broken and a contrite heart. Cf. Ps. 51:17; 34:18; Matt. 11:29; Eph. 4:2. It is the characteristics of the person who does not claim any merit before God, and who when his own personal interests are at stake, "takes joyfully the spoiling of his possessions, knowing that he has a better possession and an abiding one." Heb. 10:34. Cf. Matt. 6:33. Yet meekness is not weakness. (Zachtmoedigheid staat niet gelijk met zoetsappigheid.) The truly meek individual fights with the strength and courage of a lion for the interests of *God's* kingdom, such as Christian education and Christian missions. Neither is meekness to be confused with "good-naturedness." Only the Christian is "meek."

2. "..... *for they shall inherit the earth.*"

To the one who "takes joyfully the spoiling of his possessions," is promised the inheritance of the earth. Cf. Ps. 37:11. Not only will he receive from God a place of honor in the *new* earth (Rev. 21:1), but according to Ps. 37, he will inherit *this* earth. He may possess only a small portion of this earth or of earthly goods, but a small portion *with God's blessing resting upon it* is more than the greatest riches without God's blessing.

> "A little that the righteous hold
> Is better far than wealth untold
>   Of many wicked men;
> Destroyed shall be their arm of pride.
> But they who on the Lord confide
>   Shall be upholden then."

The word "inherit" indicates that:

(*a*) By grace the citizen of the kingdom has a *right* to this possession;

(*b*) He will *certainly* receive it;

(*c*) He will not need to *earn* it himself.

QUESTION FOR DISCUSSION. Just what comfort do the first three beatitudes give us in this period of crisis?

REFERENCES

[1] R. C. TRENCH, *Synonyms of the N. T.*, pp. 120, 121, 122.

[2] R. C. TRENCH, op. cit., pp. 222, 223.

[3] E. Y. MULLINS, art. "Paraclete" in *I. S. B. E.*; A. T. ROBERTSON, *Grammar of the N. T.*, p. 66; A. DEISSMANN, *Light from the Ancient East*, pp. 153, 187, 222, 307, 336.

READING AND STUDY HELPS

1. See the works mentioned in Outline I.

2. For the Beatitudes I know of nothing better than J. Oswald Dykes, *The Beatitudes of the Kingdom*, pages 25-80.

3. For the meaning of individual terms see R. C. Trench, *Synonyms of the N. T.*

4. On Barthianism see Outline 9, *Christ's Parting Words*, FEDERATION MESSENGER, Nov., 1933. Also for literature.

CHAPTER IV

THE CITIZENS OF THE KINGDOM: THEIR CHARACTER AND BLESSEDNESS

(The Beatitudes)

MATTHEW 5:6-12.
"Blessed are they that hunger and thirst after righteousness: for they shall be filled. Blessed are the merciful: for they shall obtain mercy. Blessed are the pure in heart: for they shall see God. Blessed are the peace-makers: for they shall be called the sons of God. Blessed are they that have been persecuted for righteousness' sake: for theirs is the kingdom of heaven. Blessed are ye when men shall reproach you, and persecute you, and say all manner of evil against you falsely, for my sake. Rejoice, and be exceeding glad: for great is your reward in heaven: for so persecuted they the prophets that were before you."

Cf. LUKE 6:21-23.
"Blessed are ye that hunger now; for ye shall be filled..... Blessed are ye when men shall hate you, and when they shall separate you from their company, and reproach you, and cast out your name as evil, for the Son of man's sake. Rejoice in that day, and leap for joy: for behold, your reward is great in heaven; for in the same manner did their fathers unto the prophets."

I. THE PROGRESS OF FAITH: THE FOURTH BEATITUDE.

A. Relation to the First Group of Beatitudes.

Out of the depths of conscious spiritual poverty, mourning over sin, and broken-heartedness, God causes the citizens of the kingdom to cry unto him for that greatest of all treasures, right-

The Sermon on the Mount 51

eousness. Cf. Ps. 130:1. From conscious want the Christian proceeds to conscious and fervent longing, not as if he did not possess as yet, but he does not yet possess *consciously*. Thus we see a progressive order: conscious want, conscious longing, conscious possession.

B. "BLESSED ARE THEY THAT HUNGER AND THIRST AFTER RIGHTEOUSNESS . . . . ."

1. *Meaning of righteousness*:

(*a*) Nothing less than perfection, Matt. 5:48, i. e., *absolute conformity in heart and conduct to God's Law; likeness to Jesus.* Cf. Matt. 5:17-20; esp. Deut. 6:25, "And it shall be a *righteousness* unto us, if we *observe to do all this commandment . . . as he hath commanded us.*"

(*b*) Relation to sin. Righteousness is the opposite of sin viewed as guilt, just as holiness is the opposite of sin viewed as pollution. Cf. I John 3:4. Righteousness is conformity to God's Law; sin is transgression of God's Law.

(*c*) Although the term "righteousness" as used in the Sermon on the Mount does not mean exactly the same thing as holiness, nor exactly the same thing as Christ's righteousness imputed to us, nevertheless it is the bud in which these two conceptions lie enclosed together.[1] It paves the way for the Pauline conception of imputed righteousness, for the righteousness of which Christ speaks is (1) given by God, cf. "they shall be filled," cf. Phil. 3:9; (2) it is wholly of grace; hence, it exceeds the righteousness of scribes and Pharisees (which was considered self-earned), Matt. 5:20, cf. Eph. 2:5, 8; (3) it is called *God's* righteousness, Matt. 6:33; cf. Paul's phrase, "not having a righteousness of mine own . . . . ," Phil. 3:9. Cf. Rom. 1:17; 5:1; Gal. 2:16; and (4) it presupposes sorrow for sin, i. e., true repentance, Lk. 18:13, 14, cf. Rom. 7:24-8:1. That Christ, nevertheless, refers not merely to forensic righteousness (a righteousness of legal state) but also to ethical righteousness (righteousness of conduct) is very plain from Matt. 5:20-48, esp. Matt. 6:1. The two are inseparable. The man who is justified by faith abounds in good works. The term "righteousness" as used by Christ is very comprehensive, embracing both the forensic and the ethical.

QUESTION FOR DISCUSSION. Pre's claim that the Gospel of the Kingdom is one Gospel; the Gospel of Paul another. See Scofield Bible, p. 1343; E. H. Moseley, *The Jew and His Destiny*, pp. 68-70. Is this true?

(*d*) Relation between righteousness of conduct and holiness. Both refer to the ethical ideal, to perfect moral conduct, but with this difference: the former views this conduct as conformity to God's Law, while the latter views it as separation from sin. The content of righteousness of conduct is perfect love to God and to the neighbor, Matt. 22:37-40.

(*e*) Relation between "righteousness" as pictured by Christ and the "righteousness of the Pharisees": the former is internal, the latter external; the former is of the heart, the latter of outward appearance only; the former is sincere, genuine, the latter is a manufactured article. Cf. Matt. 5:20-6:18.

The Sermon on the Mount

2. *Hunger and Thirst.* Not the person who merely feels that "something is wrong," but only he who stedfastly and intensely pursues after righteousness shall be filled. Thirst especially for people in the East means intense desire. This desire is emphasized by the addition of hunger. Cf. Ps. 42:1, "As the heart panteth after the water-brooks . . . ." Cf. Is. 55:1; 69:10; Amos 8:11; John 4:34; 6:35; 7:37; etc.

C. " . . . . . For They Shall Be Filled."

1. Christ himself is the True Bread and the Living Water which satisfies this longing. Cf. John 4:14; 6:48.

2. "Filled" means satisfied with food. It is derived from a word meaning pasture, grass.

3. How is this hunger and thirst after righteousness filled? Answer: (1) By the imputation of Christ's merits. Thus we obtain a righteousness of state: (2) By the sanctifying work of the Holy Spirit. Thus we obtain a righteousness of inner condition and outward conduct. Cf. Rom. 8:3-5; II Cor. 3:18. This sanctifying work of (or "filling" by) the Holy Spirit is a gradual process, not completed till death.

II. THE PERFECTION OF FAITH: THE FIFTH, SIXTH, AND SEVENTH BEATITUDES.

A. Relation of These Three to the Former and To Each Other.

These three beatitudes describe the righteousness with which the hungry and thirsty soul is filled, i. e., they give us three characteristics of this righteousness: mercy, purity of heart, and peace-making. Some see a relation of correspondence or parallelism between the beatitudes of conscious want and those of conscious possession: between the first and fifth, the second and sixth, the third and seventh. This scheme impresses us as being arbitrary. The real relation is most probably one of organic growth (like in the first group). The believer having been filled with righteousness in turn is merciful to others (fifth beatitude), cf. Lk. 6:36; Eph. 4:32; I John 4:19; he becomes conscious of the fact that his mercy is still mingled with sin; hence, he strives after purity of heart (sixth beatitude); this is followed by peace-making, according to the rule that "the wisdom which is from above is *first pure, then peaceable,*" James 3:17 (seventh beatitude): the one who has peace wishes to impart peace to others. Jesus probably selected these three virtues because they contrasted most piquantly with the "righteousness of the Pharisees." Cf. Matt. 5:20.

B. FIFTH BEATITUDE.

1. *"Blessed are the merciful . . . . ."*

(a) Mercy is love for those in misery and a forgiving spirit toward the sinner. It embraces both the kindly feeling and the kindly act. We see it exemplified in the Good Samaritan, Luke 10, and especially in Christ, the merciful High Priest, Heb. 2:17.

(b) It is a peculiarly Christian virtue. Romans put their old and infirm slaves on an island and allowed them to perish. They spoke of four cardinal virtues: wisdom, justice, temperance, and courage;[2] they did not include mercy. Cf. Prov. 12:10.

2. *"For they shall obtain mercy."*

(*a*) Nevertheless, God's mercy is always first (cf. fourth and fifth beatitudes), Eph. 4:32.

(*b*) For the character of divine mercy see Num. 14:18; II Sam. 24:14; Ps. 86:5; 103:8; 45:8; I Pet. 1:3, etc.

(*c*) Only those who are merciful obtain mercy. Cf. Matt. 18:21-35; Matt. 6:12, 14, 15; Jas. 2:13.

QUESTION FOR DISCUSSION. We have said that being merciful is a peculiarly Christian virtue. Is this true? Think of all the "mercy" manifested by worldlings during this present crisis!

C. SIXTH BEATITUDE.

1. *"Blessed are the pure in heart . . . ."*

Pure means simple, without fold; it refers to moral wholeness or *integrity*: gold is pure when it has been separated from all foreign matter; pure in heart are those whose words and deeds correspond to the disposition of the heart; *pure* is opposed to *false*.[3] The expression "the pure" does not mean "the holy" or "the sinless" here. Jesus does not mean that any one can be *sinless* in and by himself; for he teaches us to pray, "Forgive us our debts." See further against perfectionism: I Kings 8:46; Prov. 20:9; Eccl. 7:20; Rom. 3:10, 12; Jas. 3:2; I John 1:8; Rom. 7:22-24; Gal. 2:20; 5:17; Phil. 3:12, 13; Ps. 32:5; 130:3; 143:2; Dan. 9:16, etc. But the expression "pure in heart" refers to *one definite virtue*, namely, *real, inner, honesty, integrity* (a *Chris-*

tian virtue); it refers to the man who is *without guile,* to the one who is "not deceitful." A comparison with the exact Hebrew equivalent will establish this point. Cf. Ps. 24:4; 73:1; Gen. 20:5, 6; I Tim. 1:5, etc.

2. "..... *For they shall see God."*

The fact that the pure *in heart* shall see God shows that not physical but moral vision is meant. Just as a person with a mean character will never be able to understand a person with a beautiful character, so the impure man will never be able to see God, the Pure One. Cf. Ps. 112:4; Prov. 4:18; John 3:3; esp. I John 3:2*b,* "We shall be *like* him for we shall *see* him even as he is." Character of this moral vision:

(*a*) It is ever a vision of God as he is mirrored in Christ; cf. John 1:14, 17, 18; II Cor. 4:6.

(*b*) Here on earth it is a vision of faith, which is "seeing in a mirror darkly," I Cor. 13:12*a*; it is a "seeing from afar," Heb. 11:13, 27. Cf. II Cor. 5:7.

(*c*) In heaven it is the sinless and uninterrupted communion of the soul with Christ, a "seeing face to face," I Cor. 13:12*b,* a "beholding of Christ's glory," John 17:24.

D. Seventh Beatitude.

1. *"Blessed are the peacemakers ....."*

This refers not to a virtue but to an activity. The Dutch has: *de vreedzamen,* the peaceable. The English translation is much better. Not men of a conciliatory disposition are meant, but those who strive to impart to others the heaven-

The Sermon on the Mount

ly blessing of peace through reconciliation with God which they themselves have received. A special Christian activity, cf. Ps. 28:3.

QUESTION FOR DISCUSSION. Why is it impossible for an unconverted person to be a peacemaker?

2. *"For they shall be called sons of God."*

Because God in Christ is the greatest Peacemaker, II Cor. 5:19; Eph. 2:14. Notice: not all men are brethren; some are children of God; others are not, I John 3:10; Romans 8:14, 17. The peacemakers are even now sons of God (by adoption, not by nature). God himself calls them thus. By and by the entire world will recognize and admit that fact, i. e., in the great Day of Judgment. Notice also that we do not read they shall be called the TEKNA, i. e., the *"children"* of God, a term of endearment; but we read, they shall be called the HUIOI, i. e., the "sons" of God, a term which expresses high honor and dignity.

QUESTION FOR DISCUSSION. Did not Christ himself come to "bring the sword"? How then can he call the peacemakers blessed?

III. THE PERSECUTION TO WHICH FAITH IS SUBJECTED: THE EIGHTH BEATITUDE.

A. "BLESSED ARE THEY THAT HAVE BEEN PERSECUTED FOR RIGHTEOUSNESS' SAKE . . . ."

This persecution will manifest itself in three ways:

1. *Hatred.* "Men shall hate you." Cf. Matt. 10:22; 24:9; Lk. 21:17; I John 3:13; John 15:19-21.

2. *Reproach.* The hatred will be revealed in words, "Men shall reproach you and say all

manner of evil against you falsely for my sake;" they "shall cast out your name as evil." So, e. g., during the early persecutions of the Church Christians were called *atheists,* because they did not worship a visible God; *immoral* because perforce they met in secret places; and *unpatriotic* because they confessed loyalty to Christ as their King and refused to worship the Roman emperor. And inasmuch as the citizen of the kingdom of darkness never understands the citizen of the kingdom of light, the former will always continue to slander the latter. Over against this hatred Christ teaches us to love even our enemies, Matt. 5:43-48.

3. *Persecution in deed,* "Men shall separate you from their company . . . . shall persecute you."

(*a*) The person who really and openly confesses his Savior suffers social ostracism. He will not be a good mixer, Matt. 27:22; John 19:15; 15:20, 21.

(*b*) This persecution may be by means of sword, fire, wild beasts, the pen, etc. It will culminate in the great tribulation, Matt. 24:21, 29; Lk. 21:12, 13; Mk. 13:19, 20; II Thess. 2, etc.

B. "REJOICE AND BE EXCEEDING GLAD: FOR GREAT IS YOUR REWARD IN HEAVEN: FOR SO PERSECUTED THEY THE PROPHETS THAT WERE BEFORE YOU."

1. *Surprising Character of this Beatitude:* The Jews generally considered all suffering (also persecution) a curse sent by God, Lk. 13:1-5, an indication of special wickedness on

the part of the sufferer. Christ reverses this with reference to those who are persecuted "for his name's sake."

2. *Reason Why the Persecuted for Christ's Name's Sake are Called Blessed:*

(*a*) Because this persecution will indicate the genuine character of their faith, "for so persecuted they the prophets . . . ." Cf. Lk. 21:13, ". . . . . it shall turn out unto you for a testimony." Cf. Matt. 23:29, 30, 31, 37; Lk. 13:34; Acts 7:52.

(*b*) Because Christian character is purged and made mature through suffering, Rom. 5:3, 4; Jas. 1:3, 4; Book of Job.

(*c*) Because persecution is followed by great reward in heaven; not a wage won by human merit, Lk. 17:10; Rom. 4:4; but a reward in proportion to, yet much greater than, the sacrifice, Rom. 8:18; II Cor. 4:17.

REFERENCES

1) G. Vos, *op. cit.*, p. 116.
2) D. S. Adam, *Handbook of Christian Ethics*, p. 84 ff.

READING AND STUDY HELPS

In this lesson the concept of righteousness is especially important, as throughout this sermon Christ opposes his own "righteousness" to that of the Pharisees. See G. Vos, op. cit., pp. 103-124; W. Geesink, *Gereformeerde Ethiek*, I, p. 453 ff.; J. Stalker, *The Ethic of Jesus*, p. 59 ff.

CHAPTER V

THE CITIZENS OF THE KINGDOM: THEIR RELATION TO THE WORLD

(The Two Emblems: Salt and Light)

MATTHEW 5:13-16.
> "Ye are the salt of the earth: but if the salt have lost its savor, wherewith shall it be salted? It is thenceforth good for nothing, but to be cast out and trodden under foot of men. Ye are the light of the world. A city set on a hill cannot be hid. Neither do men light a lamp, and put it under a bushel, but on a stand; and it shineth unto all that are in the house. Even so let your light shine before men; that they may see your good works, and glorify your Father who is in heaven."

I. CONNECTION WITH THE FOREGOING VERSES.

In the Beatitudes the character and blessedness of the *citizens* of the kingdom was described. The last beatitude was transitional in character. It described the attitude of the world toward the citizens of the kingdom. The Two Emblems describe the opposite, namely, the influence of the kingdom upon the world. Though Christ's disciples are hated by the world, nevertheless, they are the salt of the earth and the light of the world.

II. THE CITIZENS OF THE KINGDOM ARE THE SALT OF THE EARTH AND THE LIGHT OF THE WORLD.

A. THE COMMON LESSON TAUGHT BY THESE EMBLEMS.

1. Both emphasize the Christian's *distinctiveness*, i. e., his spiritual separation from the world. Just as salt differs from the saltless, and light contrasts with darkness, so the citizens of the kingdom differ strikingly from the children of the world. Cf. I John 2:15; Rom. 12:2. Root of this difference: the citizens of the kingdom have received the principle of regeneration: a new life; the others have not. This Christian distinctiveness implies:

(*a*) that the citizens of the kingdom *abstain from worldly institutions and practices:* think of the movie as it exists today, dancing, gambling, murder, stealing, etc.;

(*b*) that they *do not cherish in their hearts and minds the evil practices of the world,* Mk. 7:21;

(*c*) that they *do not SET THEIR HEART on those practices which are legitimate in themselves, nor on the whole circle of earthly goods which is in itself neither good nor bad:* buying and selling, food and clothing, gold and silver, I Cor. 7:31 (A. S. V.); and

(*d*) that they *do not associate on terms of most intimate communion with the people of the world,* Ps. 1:1; II Cor. 6:15.

Only when light remains light does it shine; only when salt does not lose its savor will it serve as a preservative and a relish. Likewise, *only when Christians maintain their distinctiveness will they be the salt of the earth, etc.*

QUESTION FOR DISCUSSION. But should not the Christian co-operate with the worldling on the basis of common grace, e. g., in the sphere of labor, business, politics, education, fighting crime, etc.?

2. Salt and light cause their distinctiveness *to be felt:* salt, by acting upon the food with which it comes into contact; light, by illumining all surrounding objects. In like manner the citizens of the kingdom cause their influence to be felt: the world is different because of their presence in it.

3. Salt and light are both very precious; in a sense, indispensable. Said Pliny, "There is nothing more useful than salt and sunshine." Similarly, by grace the citizens of the kingdom are "precious," and in a sense they are "indispensable" to the world. "De kerk is de kurk waarop de wereld drijft."

QUESTION FOR DISCUSSION. Does God preserve the world only because of the presence of the church in it, or does the world serve a purpose entirely apart from the church?

B. THE SENSE IN WHICH THE TWO EMBLEMS DIFFER.

1. Salt has *especially* a *negative* function: to preserve from decay. It pictures the citizens of the kingdom in their struggle against moral deterioration. Light has a *positive* function: to fill with luster. It refers to Christians in their zeal to promote truth, beauty, and goodness, i. e., to spread the Gospel.

2. Salt acts *secretly.* You know that it prevents decay, but you cannot see it perform its work. Light shines *openly, publicly.* Similarly, Christians are both a salt, influencing the world

by means of their inner character, life, and prayers; and a light, acting upon the world by means of missionary endeavor and outward works to God's glory.

QUESTION FOR DISCUSSION. In order that we may be better able to fulfil our mission of being a salt and a light, would it not be well for our denomination to seek organic union with other Reformed and Presbyterian denominations?

III. THE CITIZENS OF THE KINGDOM ARE THE SALT OF THE EARTH.

A. "YE ARE THE SALT OF THE EARTH."

1. "Ye are the SALT of the earth." Salt has four well-known characteristics: whiteness (hence, symbolical of purity), pungency, flavor, and preservative power. In view of the context it would seem that Christ has reference to the last quality: *salt is a preservative, preventing decay.* This seems to be the "third of comparison," for it will not do to apply to Christians all that can be said about salt or about light. As salt prevents physical decay, so Christians combat spiritual decay.

QUESTION FOR DISCUSSION. Is your Society a salting salt? Are you as a group doing anything in the way of opposing corruption in government? What is your attitude toward a Christian Voters' League? Toward the desecration of the Sabbath in your community? Toward Christian Labor Organizations? Does prayer accompany all your efforts?

2. "*YE* are the salt of the earth." The word *YE* receives emphasis. It has the meaning "Ye *alone.*" The reference is to all true disciples of Jesus: the ten righteous persons whom God sought in Sodom, Gen. 18:32; the seven thou-

sand in Elijah's time, I Kings 18:18; the Waldenses in southern France and Italy, etc. Today, while loathsome wickedness openly flaunts itself, and men trample upon the palmary institutions of God, it is our duty to raise our voices in solemn and united protest.

3. "Ye are the salt of the EARTH," i. e., of "the land." In order to be a salt to the whole world we must first be a salt in our own country and in our own vicinity; and in order to be a salt anywhere we must first "have salt in ourselves," Mk. 9:50.

4. "Ye ARE the salt of the earth. Not: *ought to be* but *are*. If you are not *salt*, you are not a *believer*. Not: ye *carry* the salt, but ye *are* the salt.

B. ". . . . BUT IF THE SALT HAVE LOST ITS SAVOR, WHEREWITH SHALL IT BE SALTED? IT IS THENCEFORTH GOOD FOR NOTHING BUT TO BE CAST OUT AND TRODDEN UNDER FOOT OF MEN."

1. "If the salt have lost its savor, wherewith shall it be made salt again?" The salt used in Palestine, obtained from marshes and lagoons or from the rocks in the neighborhood of the Dead Sea, would become insipid when exposed to rain or sun.[1] Before his very eyes Christ saw many Pharisees who advocated a formal, legalistic religion in the place of the true religion of their fathers. The salt had lost its flavor in the religious life of Israel. Many children of the kingdom would be cast out. Just as salt which has lost its flavor cannot be restored to its for-

mer condition, so as a rule those who were trained in the knowledge of the truth but have resolutely set themselves against it and have become hardened in their opposition, are not renewed unto repentance. Cf. Heb. 6:4-6.

IV. THE CITIZENS OF THE KINGDOM ARE THE LIGHT OF THE WORLD.

A. "Ye Are the Light of the World."

1. "Light" in Scripture means *true knowledge of the Gospel* when it refers to the mind, Matt. 6:22, 23; it means *holiness* when it refers to the heart, Eph. 5:8, 9; and it means *joy, gladness,* when it refers to the emotions, Isa. 60:19.[2)] Accordingly, the statement, "Ye are the light of the world" means that the citizens of the kingdom are the means used by God to guide the children of the world unto the true, saving knowledge of God, unto real holiness, and unto lasting joy.

2. Notice that Christ says, "Ye are *the light*." Not, "Ye are lights." Christ is speaking of the citizens of the kingdom *as a group*.

3. However, Christians are never a light in and by themselves. They are light *"in the Lord,"* Eph. 5:8. Chrsit is the true Light, Ps. 27:1; 36:9; 43:3; Is. 49:6; 60:1; Lk. 2:32; John 8:12; 9:5; 12:35, 36, 46; II Cor. 4:6, etc. Christ is the light *lighting,* John 1:9; we are the light *lighted*. He is the sun, we the moon, reflecting the light of the sun. *If and whenever we separate ourselves from the true light, Christ, we shall not be able to shine. God imparts his light*

to us especially by means of the Word and the sacraments. Only as long as we remain in living, close, and active contact with the true Light, can we be the light to others. Cf. John 15:4, 5.

QUESTION FOR DISCUSSION. People try to justify themselves when moving to a community in which there is no sound church. They will say that they go there in order to be a light to the people in that community. As a general rule, is that reasoning correct? If we withhold from our children a positively Christian education and thus separate them from the true Light, will they shine as little sunbeams?

Remember: your electric bulb or incandescent lamp does not emit light all by itself. It imparts light only when "connected," so that the electric current generated in the power-house can be transmitted to it. Similarly, Christians are a light *"in the Lord."*

4. ". . . . . light of the *world.*" Greek: *kosmos*. Meaning: (*a*) arrangement, I Peter 3:3; (*b*) the earth, Matt. 4:8; (*c*) the human race as an organism, John 3:16; (*d*) the whole circle of earthly goods, I John 2:16; and (*e*) in our passage it refers to the ungodly multitude. Christians are a light shining in the darkness, leading the world, i. e., *sinners,* to Christ.

B. "A CITY SET ON A HILL CANNOT BE HID. NEITHER DO MEN LIGHT A LAMP, AND PUT IT UNDER A BUSHEL, BUT ON THE STAND . . . EVEN SO LET YOUR LIGHT SHINE BEFORE MEN . . . ."

1. Saying this, Christ *may have* pointed to the city of Safed, on top of a hill, shimmering in sunshine. Said John Wesley, "As well may men think to hide a city, as to hide a Christian;

The Sermon on the Mount

yea, as well may they conceal a city set upon a hill, as a holy, zealous, active lover of God and man.[4]

2. Original, ". . . . neither do men light a lamp (i. e., earthen saucer with oil and wick) and put it under an earthen peck-measure." Complete darkness would result. The "houses" to which Christ referred had only one room; hence, when placed on a stand the lamp would shine to *all that were in the house.*

3. Notice: Jesus does not say, "Even so let your light shine before men that they may *hear your good words,* but that they may *see your good works.*

QUESTION FOR DISCUSSION. Does not Jesus contradict himself? Here he tells the disciples to let their light so shine *that men may see their good works;* while in Matthew 6:1, 5, 16 he condemns the Pharisees for praying, fasting, etc., *to be seen of men.*

4. ". . . . and glorify your Father who is in heaven." Not: and glorify *you.* The glory of the Father was Christ's highest aim, John 17:4. It should be our highest aim, I Cor. 10:31; Eph. 3:21; Phil. 4:20; I Tim. 1:17; II Tim. 4:18; Heb. 13:21; I Peter 5:10; II Peter 3:18; Rev. 21:26.

REFERENCES

[1] Cf. DR. THOMAS, *The Land and the Book,* pp. 381, 382; PELOUBET, *Suggestive Illustrations on the Gospel of Matthew,* p. 84. GROSHEIDE and LENSKI give a different explanation. According to Lenski when Jesus speaks of salt losing its savor he refers to that which never actually happens or can happen. Says Lenski, "The very idea of salt losing its saltness! But that is what happens with Christians, the spiritual salt of the earth. . . . Both ideas

are beyond nature — salt losing its saltiness and having it restored again." We prefer the older explanation, however, for the following reasons:

a. Jesus does not say, "It *would* thenceforth be good for nothing," but "it *is* thenceforth good for nothing." He seems to be speaking about things which actually occur and were known to occur;

b. This is not a contrary-to-fact condition, for in the protasis we have EAN with the subjunctive; in the apodosis the future passive indicative. Cf. A. D. BURTON, *N. T. Moods and Tenses*, par. 250; A. T. ROBERTSON, *A Grammar of the N. T. in the Light of Hist. Research*, 1016, 1019;

c. The fact that *one* thing is mentioned here which is beyond nature (salt regaining its savor) does not in any way prove that also in the other thing (salt losing its savor) is beyond nature or contrary-to-fact;

d. We grant indeed that Jesus at times uses a figure "from what does not actually occur in nature," to use Lenski's own words. But in these cases Jesus generally indicates very plainly that the figure used is contrary to nature. Cf. "wherewith shall it be salted?" with "what man is there of you who, if his son shall ask him for a loaf, will give him a stone?" But Jesus does *not* say, "Who ever heard of salt losing its savor?" There is nothing in the original at all to suggest that this is a figure contrary-to-fact. If Jesus had meant it thus, he could have easily indicated it;

e. The fact that a certain kind of salt obtained from marshes, lagoons, etc., in Palestine would actually lose its savor was well known to the people to whom Christ spoke. We see no reason, therefore, to depart from the more usual explanation of these words.

2) Cf. H. BAVINCK II, p. 182.

3) Cf. YOUNG'S *Concordance* and THAYER'S *Grk. English Lexicon*.

4) WESLEY, *Works*, vol. I, p. 215.

READING AND STUDY HELPS

Consult the various works on the Sermon on the Mount which were mentioned in the first chapter. Consult articles in *I. S. B. E.*, etc., on "salt" and "light." Dr. T. P. Kaiser's book, *The Law in the Light of the Gospel*, contains two very fine sermons on the verses discussed in this chapter. See the meditation, *The Lamp on the Lampstand*, by the Rev. J. M. Ghysels in *The Banner* of August 26, 1932. See H. Bavinck, Vol II, p. 182. See J. J. Ulrich, *De Bergpredikatie*, pp. 408-591 of first vol., almost two hundred pages on these verses. Also A. Kuyper, *De Gemeene Gratie*, II, p. 681.

CHAPTER VI

THE RIGHTEOUSNESS OF THE KINGDOM

(In Harmony with the Law)

MATTHEW 5:17-19.
> "Think not that I came to destroy the law or the prophets: I came not to destroy, but to fulfil. For verily I say unto you, Till heaven and earth pass away, one jot or one tittle shall in no wise pass away from the law, till all things be accomplished. Whosoever therefore shall break one of these least commandments, and shall teach men so, shall be called least in the kingdom of heaven: but whosoever shall do and teach them, he shall be called great in the kingdom of heaven."

I. CONNECTION WITH MATTHEW 5:1-16.

A new section begins here. Up to this point Jesus has been speaking about the *citizens* of the kingdom: their character, blessedness, and relation to the world. Jesus now begins to speak about the *righteousness* of the kingdom. For the meaning of this term we refer you to Chapter IV, B. Jesus first emphasizes that the righteousness of the kingdom is in complete harmony with the law, Matt. 5:17-19; secondly, that it does not harmonize with the traditional, Jewish *interpretation* of the law, Matt. 5:20-48; thirdly, he points out the essence of this righteousness with respect to our relation to *God*, namely, the secret devotion of the heart, Matt. 6:1-18, and undivided trust in God, Matt. 6:19-34, i. e., loving God above all; and finally,

Jesus describes the essence of this righteousness with respect to our relation to *man,* namely, the absence of a censorious attitude, discrimination in judgment, in a word, *love,* i. e., loving one's neighbor as one loves himself, Matt. 7:1-12. See Chapter II, *II.*

II. THE MEANING OF THESE VERSES.

A. "Think Not That I Came to Destroy the Law or the Prophets: I Came Not to Destroy but to Fulfil."

1. We can perhaps best paraphrase this sentence as follows, "Do not begin to think,[1] as some of you are already thinking,[2] that I came to destroy the law or the prophets . . . ." "Do not begin to think," says Jesus. This was a warning. Jesus was going to say many things about the law which might be interpreted to mean that he had come to do away with the law altogether. Hence, this warning in advance. But this warning also contained an answer to the accusations which some of the multitude (namely, the Pharisees) had already advanced against Jesus. They had accused him of breaking the law with respect to the sabbath, John 5:16, 18. Jesus repudiates this charge.

2. The words, "Think not that I *came,*" definitely point to Christ's pre-existence. He existed before he came on earth, John 1:1; 8:58.

3. ". . . to destroy the law and the prophets." The words, "the law and the prophets," or "the law of Moses, the prophets, and the psalms," indicate *the entire Old Testament.* Lk. 16:16;

16:29, 31; 24:27, 44. In these expressions the word "law" refers especially to the *precepts* which are found in the O. T., and summarized in the Ten Commandments, while the term "prophets" refers especially to the *prophecies* of the Old Testament.

4. "I came not to destroy but to fulfil." The final aim of Christ's work on earth was not destructive but constructive: to save a people unto himself. Moreover, Jesus came to fulfil *the law and the prophets* in a threefold sense:

(a) He came *to fulfil the types and prophecies found in the Old Testament*. He speaks of "accomplishing" (Matt. 5:18) what had been predicted concerning him. Lk. 24:26, 27.

QUESTION FOR DISCUSSION. Books have been published of late claiming that we are *now* living in an era in which many of the Old Testament prophecies are being fulfilled (e. g., Ezek. 37:21; Nahum 2:3, 4; Isa. 19:23, etc.). Is that view correct?

(b) He came *to satisfy the demands of the law by his active and passive obedience, thereby delivering us from the curse of the law*. Jesus speaks about the "doing" of the law in verse 19. He refers to specific commandments, vss. 21, 27, etc.

(c) He came *to give us the true, spiritual interpretation of the law, i. e., to re-interpret the law: to teach men its true, deep meaning*. This both by his example and by his teaching.[3]

B. "FOR VERILY I SAY UNTO YOU, TILL HEAVEN AND EARTH PASS AWAY, ONE JOT OR ONE TITTLE SHALL IN NO WISE PASS AWAY . . . TILL ALL THINGS BE ACCOMPLISHED. WHOSOEVER, THEREFORE, SHALL

BREAK ONE OF THE LEAST OF THESE COMMANDMENTS, AND SHALL TEACH MEN SO, SHALL BE CALLED LEAST IN THE KINGDOM OF HEAVEN: BUT WHOSOEVER SHALL DO AND TEACH THEM, HE SHALL BE CALLED GREAT IN THE KINGDOM OF HEAVEN."

1. "For verily I say unto you." Thus Jesus introduces those statements which are of the greatest importance. Hence, what Jesus says here about the law should not be lightly pushed aside.

2. "Till heaven and earth pass away . . . ." Cf. Lk. 16:17. Jesus does not mean that the law will have no more value after heaven and earth have passed away. Real meaning: Just as heaven and earth seem to abide forever, even so the law will abide forever. The law, as interpreted by Christ, will *never* pass away, for in Lk. 21:33 we read, "Heaven and earth shall pass away: *but my words shall not pass away.*"

3. "One jot or one tittle shall in no wise pass away . . ." A "jot" refers to a very small Hebrew letter, a little hook which was sometimes omitted in writing. A "tittle" is the little projection which serves to distinguish Hebrew letters of similar appearance. It resembles the little line that serves to distinguish a G from a C. Goodspeed translates as follows, ". . . . not one dotting of an 'i' or crossing of a 't' . . ." The meaning is evident: not a single line of the O. T. has lost its value for us.

QUESTION FOR DISCUSSION. But has not the *ceremonial* law lost all its value for us?

4. "Whosoever, therefore, shall break one of these least commandments . . . ." The Jews distinguished between great, little, and least commandments. Jesus here teaches that not even those that were considered the very least have lost their validity.

5. ". . . . and shall teach men so, shall be called the least in the kingdom of heaven." To break the commandments is bad; *but to teach others that those commandments have no more value for us is even worse.* The reward of those who do so will not be as great as will be the reward of those who observe and teach the law out of gratitude. The term "kingdom of heaven" is here "redeemed universe" (see Outline II, B, 2, *c*).

6. ". . . . but whosoever shall do and teach them." Notice: *do* and teach. To *do* the law is even more important than to teach it; or, shall we say: *doing* the law is the best way to teach it to others"?

7. ". . . . *least* in the kingdom of heaven . . . *great* in the kingdom of heaven." There are degrees of glory as well as degrees of punishment. See Dan. 12:3; Lk. 12:47, 48; I Cor. 15:41, 42; Rev. 20:12, *b*. Esp. Matt. 18:1-4; Matt. 19:30—20:16.

III. TWO IMPORTANT CONCLUSIONS DERIVED FROM THESE VERSES.

A. THAT THE BIBLE IS ONE BOOK: The O. T. and the N. T. belong together.

Jesus clearly implies this. According to his

teaching in these verses the N. T. is the fulfilment of the Old. The Old Testament (laws and prophets) is not abrogated. There are those who maintain that the O. T. (or the O. T. plus Matthew or all of the Gospels, Acts, Epistle of James, and part of Revelation) is for the *Jews*, while the N. T. (or part of it) is for the *church*. According to the teaching of Jesus, "The New is in the Old contained; the Old is by the New explained. The New is in the Old concealed; the Old is by the New revealed."

B. That Those Are Clearly Wrong Who Say That We Have Nothing To Do With the Law.

1. The teaching of the Pre's concerning the law. Many Pre's maintain that "the law is not the rule of life for the Christian"; that "the mixture of law and grace is an evil mixture"; that *"the law was given not that it might be kept but that it might be transgressed"* (!); that the lawdispensation lasted till the death of Christ, so that we have nothing to do with the law now.[4] They base this theory upon a wrong exegesis of Rom. 6:14; Rom. 7:4, 6; Gal. 3:25, etc. Over against this false teaching we place the words of Jesus, "For verily I say unto you, Till heaven and earth pass away," etc. To be sure, the law is no longer for us *a way of salvation,* Rom. 3:20; Gal. 3:11-13; neither a *curse,* Gal. 3:13; neither do we as Christians need to observe the *outward forms* of the ceremonial law. Nevertheless, we are under the law because we are *creatures,* Rom. 2:15; Ps. 103:20; because we are still *sin-*

ners; and because we are *Christians,* saved by grace, hence required to observe the law *out of gratitude,* I Cor. 9:21.

2. N. T. passages which harmonize with the words of Jesus and which clearly show that the Premillennial view is wrong:

(*a*) The ten commandments are enjoined upon Christians in the N. T. Mk. 10:19-22; Rom. 7:7; Rom. 13:8-10; Col. 3:9; I John 5:21; James 2:8-13; 5:12, etc.

(*b*) According to the N. T. *we are under the law,* I Cor. 9:21; *we consent to the law,* Rom. 7:16; *we delight in the law,* Rom. 7:22; *we serve the law,* Rom. 7:25; *we establish the law,* Rom. 3:31; *we fulfil the law,* Rom. 13:10; Gal. 6:2; James 2:8; Rom. 8:4; *the law is in our mind,* Heb. 8:10; *the law is in our hearts,* Heb. 10:16; and (out of gratitude) *we should keep the law,* James 2:10. Surely, the words of Jesus are true. The law holds for us.

QUESTION FOR DISCUSSION. Is the hymn *Free From the Law* Biblical? Does it express the *full truth* or only one aspect of the truth concerning our relation to the law? Why is the Premillennialistic teaching concerning the law dangerous?

REFERENCES

[1] See GROSHEIDE, op. cit., p. 54; STALKER, op. cit., p. 62; BURGESS AND BONNER, *El. Grk.,* p. 152; A. T. ROBERTSON, *Grammar of N. T. Grk.,* fourth ed., pp. 853, 932.

[2] See A. T. ROBERTSON, *Commentary on Matthew,* p. 96; ABBOTT, *Commentary on Matthew,* p. 88. Also LENSKI, op. cit., in loco.

[3] This threefold meaning of "fulfilling the law" is beautifully set forth by GROSHEIDE, op. cit., p. 54.

4) Cf. HALDEMAN, *The Kingdom of God*, pp. 136, 141. *Grace and Glory*, Nov., 1930, p. 9, p. 11. A. W. PINK, *The Law and the Saint*, p. 4, etc.

READING AND STUDY HELPS

A. T. Robertson, *The Pharisees and Jesus*, Chaps. 1 and 2; W. Geesink, *Gereformeerde Ethiek*, I, pp. 453, 454, 463; T. P. Kaiser, *The Law in the Light of the Gospel;* H. Bavinck, I, p. 409 ff.; II, p. 416, p. 600; III, p. 131 ff.; IV, p. 491 ff. Various commentaries previously mentioned. Article "Law in the N. T." in *I. S. B. E.* G. C. Aalders, *De Profeten des Ouden Verbonds*, Chap. 13.

CHAPTER VII

THE RIGHTEOUSNESS OF THE KINGDOM
(Versus the Traditional Jewish Interpretation of the Law)
Jesus and the Pharisees

MATTHEW 5:20.
"For I say unto you, that except your righteousness shall exceed the righteousness of the scribes and Pharisees, ye shall in no wise enter into the kingdom of heaven."

I. CONNECTION WITH THE PRECEDING VERSES.

In the verses which we studied in the last Chapter, Jesus pointed out the great importance and abiding validity of the law. In the verse which we discuss now Jesus says, as it were, that since the law is so precious it should be recognized in its deeply spiritual significance, and one should not be satisfied with a merely outward keeping of the law, i. e., with the righteousness of the scribes and Pharisees.

II. MEANING OF THIS VERSE.

A. "For I say unto you."

Compare the words "Verily I say unto you" of verse 18. Jesus employs these words because he is going to make a very astounding and startling statement, a deliberate statement, a statement which will constitute the basis of nearly all the rest of the sermon. Jesus is going to

The Sermon on the Mount 79

place his own "righteousness" over against the "righteousness" of scribes and Pharisees. Now the scribes and Pharisees were the religious leaders of that time. Yet without any hesitancy or any attempt to compromise in any way Jesus is going to condemn not only the teaching but also the practice of these leaders. The boldness of Christ's remarks appears very clearly. They must have made a profound impression upon the audience.

B. ". . . . THAT EXCEPT YOUR RIGHTEOUSNESS SHALL EXCEED THE RIGHTEOUSNESS OF THE SCRIBES AND PHARISES . . . ."

1. "Your righteousness." Meaning: your conformity with the law of God, your ethical ideal, your goal in life. One's goal in life should be to love God above all and the neighbor as himself. That is what God's law demands. Moreover, that righteousness must proceed from the heart and appear in deeds.

2. ". . . . shall exceed." Scribes and Pharisees gloried in their righteousness. They considered themselves very righteous, very pious, Lk. 18:11, 12. They conceived of their righteousness in a quantitative fashion, i. e., they *counted* their good works. Cf. Matt. 19:20, "All these things have I observed; *what lack I yet?*" (a Pharisaic *spirit*, to be sure); Lk. 18:12, "I fast *twice a week*, I give *tithes* of all that I possess." Jesus now meets these Pharisees on their own ground, as it were; using their own language, he emphasizes the fact that the righteousness of the scribes and Pharisees is always

"short" of perfection. It always "lacks something." Cf. Mk. 10:21, "One thing thou *lackest*." Hence, he says, "Except your righteousness shall *exceed the measure of*[1) the righteousness of the scribes and Pharisees, ye shall in no wise enter," etc. If one thinks that he can earn heaven by means of his good works, he will soon find out that there are never enough good works. The conclusion to which the words of Jesus lead is that the quantitative conception of righteousness is wrong. The righteousness of the disciples must be *of a different kind altogether* than the righteousness of scribes and Pharisees.

3. ". . . . the righteousness of the scribes and Pharisees." The scribes are often mentioned in connection with the Pharisees. During the O. T. period the priests were at the same time the scholars and guardians of the law. But during the period between the Old and the New Testament this gradually changed, and a separate profession of "scribes" arose. This change was due to two causes: the people had been led into captivity because of their disobedience to the law; hence, in the lands of the exile they learned to esteem the law, and demanded a class of scholars who would devote themselves exclusively to its study and interpretation; secondly, during this same intertestamentary period the priests began to turn their attention to paganistic culture, thus neglecting the law, arousing the scribes to opposition. Now at first these scribes were mere copyists; later on they became students and teachers of the law; hence,

interpreters: lawyers. They held undisputed sway over the thought of the people. In the N. T. they are called "lawyers," Matt. 22:35; "doctors of the law," Lk. 5:17; "scribes," Matt. 5:20, etc. The people bestowed high honors upon them, calling them "rabbi," i. e., "my lord"; further, "teacher," Matt. 8:19; "father," Matt. 23:9, etc. They were proud, and demanded that their students should honor them even more than one honors his parents. They loved the position of first rank, Matt. 23:6; they wore tunics, Mk. 12:3; and they expected the special honor of the people in the form of the "salutations in the marketplaces," Lk. 20:46. Although the scribes pretended to give instruction in the law free of charge, they practiced fraudulent methods by which they secured exorbitant fees. Cf. Mk. 12:40; Lk. 20:47.

QUESTION FOR DISCUSSION. What is the teaching of the Gospels in regard to remuneration for Gospel workers? In how far is that teaching applicable to conditions as they exist today? Cf. Matt. 10:8, 10; Lk. 10:7; cf. I Cor. 9:14, etc.

Most of the scribes belonged to the Pharisaic class. Reason: the Pharisees recognized the "traditions" or "law-interpretations" of the scribes. The latter taught the Old Testament plus their own interpretation of it: a second Bible covering up the first.[2] They would in many instances regard the "tradition" as more binding than the written law. There were also scribes of the Sadducees; this seems to be implied in Mk. 2:16; Lk. 5:30; Acts 23:9. We are now better able to understand what Christ

meant by "the righteousness of the scribes . . ."
It was "self-righteousness": it was the attempt
to earn heaven by means of a display of so-
called good works; which did not proceed from
faith but from love of admiration; which were
not done according to God's law, but according
to an erroneous interpretation of the law; and
which did not have for their purpose the glory
of God but the glory of the scribes themselves.
No wonder that Jesus said, ". . . . except your
righteousness shall exceed the righteousness of
the scribes, ye shall in no wise enter into the
kingdom of heaven."

QUESTION FOR DISCUSSION. The scribes were convinced that the law of God needed *interpretation*. Was this idea wrong as such? Today there are those who tell us that the Bible explains itself, and needs no interpretation. What element of truth and what element of error is there in this view?

The scribes, accordingly, were a profession.
The Pharisees, however, were a sect. The name
"Pharisee" means Separatist. The Pharisees
were very careful to "separate" themselves from
the common people, from Samaritans, from
heathen, etc. Their original name was "Saints,"
later "Separatists." They constituted the patri-
otic party among the Jews, and hated the foreign political yoke. They believed in the exist-
ence of angels, in the immortality of the soul,
and in the resurrection of the body. The Sadducees denied all this. The "righteousness" of
the Pharisees was external. It consisted in the
scrupulous observance of the "traditions," i. e.,
meats and drinks and divers washings; tithing

The Sermon on the Mount

of mint, anise, and cummin. They regarded these "traditions" which had been added to the law of God by the scribes as the real Bible, as having been given by Moses to the elders, and by them transmitted orally to the people. With Christ it was the "heart" that must be right with God, not merely the "external actions." The righteousness of the Pharisees was "self-righteousness." Jesus condemned the Pharisees because of their:

a) spiritual blindness, John 3:1-14; Matt. 13:13-17; Mk. 4:12; Lk. 8:10; John 6:44, 64 ff.; Matt. 15:12-20; 16:1-4; Mk. 8:11-13; John 9:40 ff.; Lk. 11:37-54;

b) formalism, Matt. 5:17—6:18;

c) self-righteousness, Lk. 18:9;

d) prejudice, John 5:40; Matt. 11:16-19; Lk. 7:29-35;

e) traditionalism, (already mentioned);

f) hypocrisy, Matt. 6:2-7; 5:15-23; Lk. 6:37-42, etc.;

g) blasphemy against the H. Spirit, Matt. 12:31-37;

h) rejection of God in rejecting Jesus, John 5:42 ff., etc.

C. ". . . . YE SHALL IN NO WISE ENTER INTO THE KINGDOM OF HEAVEN."

Notice the difference: in verse 19 Jesus has said, "Whosoever shall break one of these least commandments and shall teach men so, shall be called *least* in the kingdom of heaven." Here:

"shall in no wise *enter* the kingdom of heaven."
Why this difference?

QUESTION FOR DISCUSSION. There are those who claim that we, as a denomination, are in danger of becoming Pharisaical. Is this true?

REFERENCES

1) Cf. THAYER'S *Lexicon*.
2) A. T. ROBERTSON, *Epochs in the Life of Jesus*, p. 67.

READING AND STUDY HELPS

See articles "Pharisees," "Scribes," in *I. S. B. E*. The book, *The Pharisees and Jesus*, by Dr. A. T. Robertson, sheds much light on this chapter, and affords easy reading.

CHAPTER VIII.

THE RIGHTEOUSNESS OF THE KINGDOM
(Versus the Traditional Jewish Interpretation of the Law)

The Sixth Commandment

MATTHEW 5:21-26.

> "Ye have heard that it was said to them of old time, Thou shalt not kill; and whosoever shall kill shall be in danger of the judgment: but I say unto you, that every one who is angry with his brother shall be in danger of the judgment; and whosoever shall say to his brother, Raca, shall be in danger of the council; and whosoever shall say, Thou fool, shall be in danger of the hell of fire. If therefore thou art offering thy gift at the altar, and there rememberest that thy brother hath aught against thee, leave there thy gift before the altar, and go thy way, first be reconciled to thy brother, and then come and offer thy gift. Agree with thine adversary quickly, while thou art with him in the way; lest haply the adversary deliver thee to the judge, and the judge deliver thee to the officer, and thou be cast into prison. Verily I say unto thee, Thou shalt by no means come out thence, till thou have paid the last farthing."

I. THE TRADITIONAL INTERPRETATION OF THE SIXTH COMMANDMENT.

A. "Ye have heard that it was said to them of old time."

1. "Ye have heard." Notice that this expression is used at the beginning of each of the five examples which Christ gives, Matt. 5:21, 27, 33, 38, and 43. Christ did not refer to the hearing

of the *reading* of the law in the synagogues. He referred to the hearing of the *interpretation* of the law as given by the scribes.

2. ". . . . that it was said to them of old time." The A. V. has "by them" instead of "to them." This "by them" is probably correct.[1]) Who were these men of old time? They were probably the "elders," etc., mentioned in the Mish. We read, "Moses received the oral law from Sinai and delivered it to Joshua, and Joshua to the elders, and the elders to the prophets, and the prophets to the men of the great synagogue." By teaching this, the scribes tried to impress upon the people that the "oral traditions" (i. e., the laws added to those which you find in the Bible) were also of divine origin. The "elders" or "the people of old time" had received them from Joshua!

B. "THOU SHALT NOT KILL; AND WHOSOEVER SHALL KILL SHALL BE IN DANGER OF THE JUDGMENT . . . ."

1. Jesus was not quoting the O. T. He was quoting the "traditional interpretation" of the sixth commandment. The scribes added to the commandment, as is evident when you compare the sixth commandment with the verse we are studying.

2. The scribes and Pharisees understood the sixth commandment to refer merely to the external crime of murder. That this was their view is clear from the words, "and whoever murders will have to answer for it in *court*"

(the real meaning according to original). They viewed as transgression of the sixth commandment only such acts of outward murder as were punishable in court. They interpreted the law *literally*. They viewed it as a mere penal code. Their righteousness was merely external, therefore.

II. CHRIST'S DEEPLY SPIRITUAL INTERPRETATION OF THE SIXTH COMMANDMENT.

A. "BUT I SAY UNTO YOU, THAT EVERY ONE WHO IS ANGRY WITH HIS BROTHER SHALL BE IN DANGER OF THE JUDGMENT."

1. Jesus sharpens the edge of every precept and searches for the principle which underlies every commandment. He points out that fundamentally this commandment against murder is a commandment against "anger," because anger is the root of murder. In comparison with the erroneous explanation given to this commandment by the scribes, the interpretation which Jesus gives may be called a *re-interpretation*. Nevertheless, it was not a new interpretation when compared to the teachings of the O. T. Cf. Lev. 19:17, 18.

QUESTIONS FOR DISCUSSION. Is anger always sinful? Every newspaper carries accounts of murder. Some suggest as a solution better laws; others, better enforcement, speedier justice, etc. Admitting the true element in all these suggestions, what is the *real* solution of the problem when viewed in the light of these words of Jesus?

2. Notice, "But *I* say unto you." Jesus does not quote from the writings of the rabbis. He speaks with authority; his own authority.

B. "... AND WHOSOEVER SHALL SAY TO HIS BROTHER, RACA, SHALL BE IN DANGER OF THE COUNCIL; AND WHOSOEVER SHALL SAY, THOU FOOL, SHALL BE IN DANGER OF THE HELL OF FIRE."

1. Jesus points out that although anger in the heart is already tantamount to murder, nevertheless, there is a gradation in sin. If the anger reveals itself outwardly, the sin deserves greater punishment. "Raca" means "simpleton," "blockhead." That the sin of unrestrained anger, i. e., an anger which reveals itself outwardly by speaking about the brother in terms of contempt is even greater in *degree* than the sin of anger in the heart (although: in *nature* the two sins are the same), Jesus makes plain by saying that while the sin of hatred as such places one in danger of the ordinary Jewish court, found in every town; the sin of venting one's wrath in words of contempt places one in danger of condemnation by the supreme council of the Jews, the Sanhedrin. Goodspeed translates, ".... and anyone who says to his brother, 'You cursed fool!' will have to answer for it in the fiery pit. "The hell of fire," literally, "the Gehenna of fire": originally derived from the Valley of Hinnom where the refuse of Jerusalem continually burned. Meaning: *love* from the heart is the fulfilment of the law; hence, when one *hates* his brother, then, even though he does not literally murder him, he has transgressed the sixth commandment, and together with it the whole law, and is subject to the divine condemnation.

III. PRACTICAL APPLICATION WHICH IS BASED UPON CHRIST'S INTERPRETATION OF THE SIXTH COMMANDMENT: THE DUTY OF RECONCILIATION.

A. "IF THEREFORE THOU ART OFFERING THY GIFT AT THE ALTAR, AND THERE REMEMBEREST THAT THY BROTHER HATH AUGHT AGAINST THEE, LEAVE THERE THY GIFT . . . FIRST BE RECONCILED TO THY BROTHER."

1. The general meaning of the entire passage is this: Pharisees may tell you that God is pleased with external offerings as such; this is not true: if, while you bring your offering, you are living in anger with your brother, the offering will not be accepted by the Lord. The Lord sees the *heart*.

2. Notice: Jesus does not say, "And there remember that you have something against the brother," but, "that the brother has something against you." Nevertheless, this does not mean what it might seem to mean to an English reader. The real sense is this: "If you remember that another brother has a *valid accusation* against you, so that not the other brother but *you yourself* are the guilty party (for example, you have called your brother a "blockhead" or an "accursed fool," see context), then you should first go and be reconciled with him. Otherwise your offering will not be acceptable."

QUESTION FOR DISCUSSION. But suppose you are not guilty. The other brother is guilty. Is it then your duty to seek reconciliation with your brother before coming to the communion-table?

B. "Agree with thine adversary quickly, while thou art with him in the way; lest haply the adversary deliver thee to the judge .. and thou be cast into prison. ...."

Jesus is still speaking (according to the context) to the offender, the one who has injured his brother by saying "Raca" or "Accursed Fool," to him. The meaning, then, is: "Be not surprised at the urgency of My command to be reconciled; for should it so be that you were to pass from this life with a heart still at variance with your brother, with a wrong still upon you for which you have not sought his forgiveness, that wrong will itself testify against you in the day of judgment. Moreover, dying with that spirit of hatred still within your heart, you will never escape from the prison of hell." We regard these words to be parabolical; not allegorical, however.

Question for Discussion. In the light of the preceding verses and of Matt. 18:15-18 and I Cor. 6:1-11, is it proper for Christians to bring suit against one another? Are there any exceptions to this rule?

REFERENCE
1) Grosheide, op. cit., p. 57.

READING AND STUDY HELPS
A. T. Robertson, *The Pharisees and Jesus*, p. 122; Tholuck, op. cit., pp. 154-204. W. Geesink, op. cit., I, 389 ff., 463 ff.; Lord's Day 40 of the *Heidelberg Catechism*. W. Geesink, *Van 's Heeren Ordinantiën*, IV, p. 174. Works on the Ten Commandments, e. g., by Golladay, Morgan, Coffin, etc. Works on H. Catechism (Lord's Day 40), such as: A. Kuyper, Sr., *E Voto;* Thelemann (translated into English), etc.

CHAPTER IX

THE RIGHTEOUSNESS OF THE KINGDOM
(VERSUS THE TRADITIONAL JEWISH INTERPRETATION OF THE LAW)

The Seventh Commandment

MATTHEW 5:27-32.

"Ye have heard that it was said, Thou shalt not commit adultery: but I say unto you, that every one that looketh on a woman to lust after her hath committed adultery with her already in his heart. And if thy right eye causeth thee to stumble, pluck it out, and cast it from thee: for it is profitable for thee that one of thy members should perish, and not thy whole body be cast into hell. And if thy right hand causeth thee to stumble, cut it off, and cast it from thee: for it is profitable for thee that one of thy members should perish, and not thy whole body go into hell. It was said also, Whosoever shall put away his wife, let him give her a writing of divorcement: but I say unto you, that every one that putteth away his wife, saving for the cause of fornication, maketh her an adulteress: and whosoever shall marry her when she is put away committeth adultery."

I. ADULTERY IN MATTERS OF WEDLOCK.

A. "YE HAVE HEARD THAT IT WAS SAID, THOU SHALT NOT COMMIT ADULTERY: BUT I SAY UNTO YOU, THAT EVERYONE THAT LOOKETH ON A WOMAN TO LUST AFTER HER HATH COMMITTED ADULTERY WITH HER ALREADY IN HIS HEART."

1. Again Jesus attacks the "righteousness" of the scribes and Pharisees. They condemned only the outward act of adultery. Indeed, they

were very severe toward those who committed literal adultery, John 8:1-11. Jesus, however, views the evil lust of the heart as adultery, just as he views the hatred of the heart as murder. God's Word condemns adultery in no uncertain terms. According to the O. T. adulterers were to be stoned, Lev. 20:10; Deut. 22:22. The prophet Nathan is sent by God to tell David, "Thou art the man." John the Baptist rebuked King Herod because he was living in continuous adultery with his brother Philip's wife, Matt. 14:4. It is of the utmost importance, therefore, that we as Christians follow the very strict teaching of Christ with respect to this sin.

QUESTION FOR DISCUSSION. Whereas the sin of adultery in the heart is so terrible, is it not our duty as Christian parents to instruct our children in regard to proper sex-relations?

B. "AND IF THY RIGHT EYE CAUSETH THEE TO STUMBLE, PLUCK IT OUT AND CAST IT FROM THEE: FOR IT IS PROFITABLE FOR THEE THAT ONE OF THY MEMBERS SHOULD PERISH, AND NOT THY WHOLE BODY BE CAST INTO HELL . . . ."

1. These words are not to be taken literally. Christ in this very sermon, even in this very passage, shows the absurdity of the literal interpretation of the commandments. Surely, it would be very inconsistent for us to insist upon a literal interpretation here. Moreover, even if one should literally pluck out his right eye, this would help but very little; he would still be able to commit adultery with his left eye. Jesus himself interprets this passage for us in Matt. 18:7-9. By the offending right hand and right

eye he means "occasions of stumbling." The meaning of the entire passage is this: One should avoid everything that will in the natural course of events lead to sin, especially, to sin against the seventh commandment.

QUESTIONS FOR DISCUSSION. How can this argument of Jesus be applied against the practice of attending the movies? Are they not institutions which cause one to stumble into immorality?

Paul's words may be taken as a commentary on this passage, "Put to death therefore your members which are upon the earth: fornication, uncleanness, passion," etc. Jesus clearly teaches that we should tear out of our hearts the lustful eye. He emphasizes that this should be done at once, not gradually. Hence, "pluck it out, cut it off!" Do not compromise with these temptations for a single moment!

II. ADULTERY IN MATTERS OF DIVORCE.

A. "IT WAS SAID ALSO, WHOSOEVER SHALL PUT AWAY HIS WIFE, LET HIM GIVE HER A WRITING OF DIVORCEMENT."

1. The teaching of the Pharisees, which Jesus here opposes, amounted to this, "Whosoever wishes to divorce his wife, let him do so for whatever cause, providing that he give her a bill of divorcement." They based this opinion on Deut. 24:1, "When a man hath taken a wife .... and it come to pass that she find no favor in his eyes, because he hath found some uncleanness in her; then let him write her a bill of divorcement." Rabbi Shammai emphasized the words, "because he hath found some unclean-

ness in her," and taught that only adultery was to be considered a ground of divorce. Rabbi Hillel emphasized the words, "...... and it come to pass that she find no favor in his eyes," and taught that a man was allowed to divorce his wife if she was not agreeable to him in every respect. This opinion prevailed. Thus, by means of this misinterpretation of the seventh commandment, the law of God was violated.

2. The "bill of divorce" read as follows (in part): "On the............day of the week............in the month...............in the year...............from the beginning of the world...............I...............the son of...................of the town of...................with entire consent of mind, and without any constraint, have divorced, dismissed, and expelled thee ....daughter of................of the town............... who hast been my wife hitherto. ....Thou art therefore free for anyone who would marry thee. Let this be thy bill of divorce from me, a writing of separation and expulsion, according to the law of Moses and Israel. ...., the son of................, witness; ...., the son of............, witness.[1)]

B. ".... BUT I SAY UNTO YOU, THAT EVERYONE THAT PUTTETH AWAY HIS WIFE, SAVING FOR THE CAUSE OF FORNICATION, MAKETH HER AN ADULTERESS: AND WHOSOEVER SHALL MARRY HER WHEN SHE IS PUT AWAY COMMITTETH ADULTERY."

1. This passage introduces us to a subject which has given rise to many questions and debates. It is not our purpose to state our opinion on some of these controversial subjects. We

The Sermon on the Mount 95

purposely refrain from doing so. We shall try, however, to prepare the reader for an intelligent discussion of the matter in general.

In order to enter into this matter intelligently it is first of all necessary to give a *correct translation* of the passage before us. This is a phase of the subject which, in our opinion, has received very scant attention. Yet, it must be evident to all that ecclesiastical decisions which do not rest upon a thorough exegetical study of the passages involved have very little, if any, value. *We must make a study of the passage under discussion in the original! We must study its context also in the original!*

Inasmuch as our own translation of this passage does not completely agree with any which we have seen so far, we have discussed this phase of the question more fully in an APPENDIX. Those who wish to make further study of this very important and most fundamental angle of the subject are therefore referred to this appendix.

It is altogether possible that the reader has often wondered what Jesus could have meant when he said, "But I say unto you that everyone that putteth away his wife, saving for the cause of fornication, *maketh HER an adulteress.*" In amazement you may have asked, "How can a wife ever become an adulteress merely because her husband sends her away? What evil has the poor woman committed?" We are neither admitting nor denying that you had the right to ask the question in this form. We believe, however, that the entire matter will become clearer when you accept a different translation of the passage than the version with which you have become familiar. In order to indicate clearly the difference between the usual translation and our own we shall place them side by side, thus:

American Revised Version:	Our own translation:
"But I say unto you, that every one that putteth away his wife, saving for the cause of fornication, **maketh her an adulteress:** and whosoever shall marry her when she is put away **committeth adultery.**"	"But I say unto you, that every one who puts away his wife, saving for the cause of fornication, **causes her to suffer adultery,** and he who shall marry her that has been put away **makes himself guilty of adultery.**"

2. It will be evident that if our translation be correct, the first part of this passage acquires a meaning altogether different from the one ordinarily given to it, while the meaning of the last clause, although not seriously affected, is also somewhat altered.

It must be remarked that in this passage Jesus is speaking about the sin of the *husband* who *divorces* his wife. We must remember that Matthew is writing for the Jews, and among the Jews the wife could not divorce the husband but the husband could divorce his wife. Among the Gentiles a wife could divorce her husband. This also is condemned by Christ, Mk. 10:12.

3. *One* thing must strike us when we study this passage in connection with its context, namely, that Christ's rule in regard to marriage and divorce is very strict and marks a striking contrast with the custom which had the approval of many of the Pharisees. Christ very clear-

ly mentions only one ground of divorce, namely, adultery. The impression is certainly conveyed that where adultery has not taken place divorce is sinful and so is subsequent marriage with another.

Whereas according to many Pharisees a married man could desire another wife, could dismiss his own wife for a trivial reason, e. g., because she did not serve a good dinner, and could marry another, *could do all this without committing adultery*, Jesus teaches that according to the divine law as found in the O. T. this man would be guilty of grievous sin all along the line:

a. he committed "adultery in his heart" when he "looked after a woman to lust after her," verse 28.

b. he sinned grievously when he "put away his wife" although she had not committed fornication, Matt. 5:32, cf. Mk. 10:11; also Matt. 19:9.

c. the wrong which his wife would suffer as a result of her husband's act was to be charged to his account. *"He causes her to suffer adultery."*

4. Moreover, as according to the law of Christ (i. e., the institution of marriage as Christ interprets it) the first marriage is still binding, the man who marries the woman divorced on a ground other than adultery also *makes himself guilty of adultery,* Matt. 5:32, *commits adultery,* Lk. 16:18.

Do not try to answer the following questions

before you have made a rather thorough study of most of the sources mentioned below.

Some of these questions are very fundamental.

QUESTIONS FOR DISCUSSION.

1. Are persons married as soon as a minister pronounces them to be "husband and wife"? Always?

2. Are persons married when they "live as man and wife"? Always?

3. Must the Church recognize (as valid) every marriage which has been consummated by the State?

4. You are now ready for this very important question: just what constitutes marriage? Is marriage the mutual and voluntary compact between a man and a woman to live together as husband and wife, followed by solemnization in accordance with the laws of the State? Is it a merely legal relationship? Or does it consist in the mutual assumption of marital rights and duties, apart from ecclesiastical or civil ceremonies (common law marriage)? Does the fact that a man and a woman live as husband and wife constitute marriage? Or does the state of marriage exist only then when the union of two persons as husband and wife does not take place in conflict with the definite statements concerning marriage and divorce which we find in Scripture? Or must we combine several of these elements in order to arrive at the correct answer to the question: what constitutes marriage?

5. According to Scripture may a man marry his deceased wife's sister?

6. According to Scripture just what constitutes incest?

7. Just what constitutes adultery? Do you agree with those who hold that "there are offences which make married life so intolerable that there can be no restoration of affection . . . and therefore, such offences might rightly be put in the same category as conjugal infidelity in the strict sense of the word"? Is "extreme cruelty" tantamount to adultery? Is it proper to give the word "adultery" this broad meaning?

8. Just what constitutes divorce? Just what constitutes re-marriage?

9. The marriage of Mr. A. and Mrs. A. is recognized by the State and by the Church. They are really "married."

Now Mr. A. commits adultery. Consequently, Mrs. A. divorces him on this Scriptural ground and she marries another. Now does it follow that also Mr. A. has the right to marry another? One says, "Surely, *that* follows, for the former marriage tie has been dissolved." Another answers, "The fact that Mrs. A. has divorced Mr. A. (on the Scriptural ground of adultery) and has married another does *not* as such give Mr. A. the right to marry another, for Christ clearly teaches that only *then* has a person the right to obtain a divorce and to re-marry when his (her) mate *commits adultery*. But in this case *Mrs. A. has not committed adultery;* hence, Mr. A. has not the right to marry another." Which of these two interpretations do you regard as the right one, and why? Or is neither one correct?

10. According to Scripture may a person divorced on a ground other than adultery ever marry another?

11. How many grounds for divorce does Scripture recognize?

12. According to Scripture, can a person who was divorced on a ground other than adultery, and who was married to another, be given the right and fellowship of membership in the Church, and if so, on which conditions?

13. What should be our attitude toward *trial marriages*?2)

14. What, according to Scripture, are the duties of the wife with respect to her husband, and of the husband with respect to his wife?

REFERENCES

1) See article, "Divorce in O. T." in *I. S. B. E.*

2) See B. B. Lindsay, *The Revolt of Modern Youth*, p. 169.

READING AND STUDY HELPS

1. Be sure to read and study the following passages: Gen. 1:27; 2:24; 38:8; Lev. 18:18-20; 20:10; 22:22; Num. 36:6, 7; Deut. 22:13 ff.; 24:1-4; Is. 50:1; Jer. 2:2; Ezek. 16:8-23; Hos. 2:19 ff.; Matt. 5:32; 14:3, 4; 19:3-10; Mk. 6:17, 18; 10:9-12; Lk. 3:19, 20; 16:18; I Cor. 7:15; Eph. 5:31-33.

2. Works on the H. Catechism and on the Ten Commandments, on the subject: the seventh commandment. See titles in former chapters.

3. D. S. Adam, *A Handbook of Christian Ethics*, pp. 248-250; W. Geesink, *Gereformeerde Ethiek*, II, pp. 283-285; T. P. Kaiser, *The Law in the Light of the Gospel*, pp. 71-83; and articles, "Adultery" and "Divorce" in the *I. S. B. E.*; J. R. Miller, *The Home Beautiful*; G. Wielenga, *Ons Huwelijksformulier*.

4. The various commentaries on Matthew and on The Sermon on the Mount mentioned in chapter 1. See especially Lenski on this passage.

5. Article "Marriage" in *Hasting's Encyclopedia of Religion and Ethics;* articles Echtscheiding (H. Bouwman), Huwelijk, Tweede Huwelijk, Huwelijksbevestiging (J. Jansen), Huwelijkssluiting (C. Lindeboom), Bloedschande (G. Keizer), in *Christelijke Encyclopaedie*.

6. Be sure to read the *Agendas and Acts of the Synods of the Christian Reformed Church*, from 1914-1932 (on this question), including the *Report of Committee on Divorce*, Part I, *Agenda*, 1932; F. Nymeyer, *Prohibited Marriages;* R. H. Charles, *The Teaching of the N. T. on Divorce*.

7. On the linguistic aspect see Charles, *The Teaching of the N. T. on Divorce*, p. 91 ff.; Robertson's *Grammar*, Young's *Concordance*, and APPENDIX.

CHAPTER X

THE RIGHTEOUSNESS OF THE KINGDOM
(VERSUS THE TRADITIONAL JEWISH INTERPRETATION OF THE LAW)

The Third Commandment: The Oath

MATTHEW 5:33-37.

> "Again, ye have heard that it was said to them of old time, Thou shalt not forswear thyself, but shalt perform unto the Lord thine oaths: but I say unto you, Swear not at all, neither by the heaven, for it is the throne of God; nor by the earth, for it is the footstool of his feet; nor by Jerusalem, for it is the city of the great King. Neither shalt thou swear by thy head, for thou canst not make one hair white or black. But let your speech be Yea, yea; Nay, nay; and whatsoever is more than these is of the evil one."

I. THE PHARISAIC INTERPRETATION OF THE OATH.

A. "AGAIN, YE HAVE HEARD THAT IT WAS SAID TO THEM OF OLD TIME . . . ."

Up to this point Jesus has been discussing the traditional interpretation of the sixth and seventh commandments. The word "Again," indicates that he is about to speak about another commandment, and that in doing so he has in mind the same general purpose, namely, opposing his own deeply spiritual interpretation of the law to the erroneous, literal interpretation of the Pharisees. The subject of the oath is related especially to the third commandment, inasmuch as an oath is an invocation of the name of God: a solemn declaration or promise with an appeal to God as Witness and, in case one has sworn falsely, as Avenger. Accordingly, perjury, i. e., the violation of an oath (de meineed), is a sin against the third commandment: "Thou shalt not take the name of Jehovah thy God in vain . . . . ." Indirectly, however, this saying of Jesus concerning the oath has reference also to the eighth commandment, for when one does not "perform unto the Lord his oaths" he steals. Finally, it is also related to the ninth commandment, for by giving false testimony against an accused in court while one is under oath, one "bears false witness against his neighbor."[1]

Hence, it is readily seen that if Jesus gives his spiritual interpretation of the law regarding the oath, he thereby indicates that the whole law should be interpreted spiritually.

For the expression, ". . . . that it was said to them of old time," see Outline VIII.

B. "Thou shalt not forswear thyself, but shalt perform unto the Lord thine oaths."

The meaning of, "Thou shalt not forswear thyself" is "Thou shalt not swear *by my name* falsely," Lev. 19:12. The Pharisees interpreted this commandment literally, and reasoned that it meant only that when one actually promised something with an oath in which the name of God was literally taken upon the lips, this promise must be kept. Very cleverly they used two passages from Scripture: Lev. 19:12 and Num. 30:2 (cf. Deut. 6:13; 23:21), in order to drive home their point. The falseness of their view becomes evident when one considers that Scripture nowhere tells us that Num. 30:2 exhausts the meaning of the law of the oath, Lev. 19:12. In order to make the law of no effect the Pharisees would encourage the people to swear by some part of the created universe, e. g., by heaven or by the earth, rather than by the name of God. In brief, they reasoned as follows, "Oaths sworn by the name of God are binding; you must perform unto the Lord your oaths; but oaths sworn by heaven or by the earth are not binding. Hence, use them as much as you wish." In this way they encouraged light and flippant swearing. Thus by means of their tradition they made the law of God of no effect.

II. CHRIST'S SPIRITUAL VIEW OF THE OATH.

A. "But I say unto you, Swear not at all.."

1. The general meaning of these words is, "You must abstain not only from actual and literal perjury, but you must do away entirely with those thoughtless, flippant, supposedly nonbinding oaths to which you are accustomed."

2. Does Jesus prohibit the use of the oath as such when he says, "Swear not at all"? Among the Waldenses, Bohemian Brethren, Mennonites and Quakers there were and are many who consider every oath unscriptural. However, this cannot be correct, for:

(*a*) In the O. T. the oath was commanded, Deut. 6:13, "Thou . . shalt swear by his name."

Cf. Isa. 65:16; Deut. 10:20; Isa. 19:18. Jesus did not come to destroy the O. T. law, Matt. 5:17.

(*b*) In the O. T. Dispensation the oath was much in use, and never as such forbidden. Oaths were sworn by Abraham, Gen. 21:34; by Abraham's servant, Gen. 24:9; by Joseph, Gen. 47:31; 50:5; by "the princes of the congregation," Josh. 9:15; by the children of Israel, Judges 21:5; by Ezra, Ezra 10:5; by Ittai, II Sam. 15:21; by Obadiah, I Kings 18:10; by all Judah and Benjamin, II Chron. 15:14, 15 ("And they sware unto Jehovah with a loud voice and with shouting and with trumpets and with cornets. And all Judah rejoiced at the oath: for they had sworn with all their heart . . ."), etc.

(*c*) The N. T. plainly teaches that the oath is permissible, Heb. 6:16.

(*d*) Paul makes frequent use of the oath, Rom. 1:9; Phil. 1:8; I Thess. 2:5; II Cor. 1:23.

(*e*) God himself "sware by himself" to confirm his covenant-promise to us. Our sense of assurance of salvation rests upon this oath of the covenant, Gen. 22:15-18; Deut. 7:8; 32:40; I Chron. 16:16; Isa. 62:8; Ps. 105:9; 106:26; Ezek. 20:5; Dan. 12:7; Jer. 11:5; Lk. 1:73; Acts 2:30, and Heb. 6:13-20.

(*f*) Jesus himself made use of the oath. He uses it in this very sermon. The expression, "Verily I say unto you," amounted to an oath, Matt. 5:18; 6:2. Moreover, by means of an oath Jesus declared that he was the Christ, the Son of God, Matt. 26:63, 64.

(*g*) An oath, moreover, characterizes the High Priesthood of Christ, Heb. 7:20-28.

Accordingly, the words, "Swear not at all . ." cannot mean that every oath is wrong. What is more natural than to explain these words in the light of their specific context? Accordingly, we arrive at the conclusion that Jesus meant:

(*a*) That the members of the church *in their relation to each other* should not use the oath at all. Cf. the words, "I say unto YOU . . . ."

(*b*) That the oath should never be used *for light and trivial reasons, e.g., in ordinary discourse or to promote merely selfish interests.* In ordinary discourse "Yes" and "No" should be sufficient. Cf. the words, "But let your speech be, Yea, yea; Nay, nay."

(*c*) That one should not try to escape the obligation of the oath-confirmed promise by *swearing by the creature instead of by the Creator.* Such oaths should not be sworn at all. Cf. the words, "Swear not at all; neither by the heaven," etc. Cf. Jas. 5:12. But if such oaths are sworn, they are binding. Be sure to study Matt. 23:16-22.

QUESTIONS FOR DISCUSSION. Under what circumstances are oaths permissible? See H. Catechism, Questions and Answers 101, 102; also A. Kuyper, E Voto III, p. 611. Mention the three traditionally recognized characteristics of a legitimate oath. Is the Chr. Reformed denomination right in its stand against oath-bound secret societies? Give reasons for your answer.

B. ". . . NEITHER BY THE HEAVEN, FOR IT IS THE THRONE OF GOD; NOR BY THE EARTH . . . ."

1. General meaning: The Pharisees are wrong when they permit you to swear by heaven

and tell you that such an oath is not binding; for heaven is glorious only because it contains the throne of God; similarly, an oath sworn by the earth is binding, for the earth is God's footstool; Jerusalem is God's city, Ps. 48:3. God is the great King. Hence, an oath sworn by heaven or by earth or by Jerusalem is an oath sworn by God.

2. "Neither shalt thou swear by thy head," i. e., you must not in swearing give your head as forfeit (onderpand), for you have no power over your own head; you cannot even make one hair white or black.

3. Instances of rash use of the oath, I Sam. 14:24, 39, 44; Mk. 6:23; Matt. 26:69-75.

QUESTION FOR DISCUSSION. In the How Book of Scouting one reads, "The Oath . . . is the backbone of the Movement." 2) Is the oath or vow of the Boy Scouts' Movement proper?

III. CHRIST URGES TRUTHFULNESS IN SPEECH IN THE PLACE OF THE COMMON USE OF THE OATH.

A. BUT LET YOUR SPEECH BE, YEA, YEA; NAY, NAY."

Meaning: Let your word be as good and as dependable as an oath; then you will not need the oath in order to confirm your statements. Do not say, "Yes" when you mean "No."

B. ". . . AND WHATSOEVER IS MORE THAN THESE IS OF THE EVIL ONE," or, "is of (or: because of) evil." The original allows either translation. According to the second interpretation the meaning would be: oaths are at times necessary because of sin, i. e., because man is by nature evil, and cannot be trusted. However, although this interpretation is grammatically permissible, it is hardly in harmony with the context. We prefer, therefore, the former view, i. e., oaths in ordinary discourse are Satan-inspired.

QUESTIONS FOR DISCUSSION. What can we do to counteract the evil of swearing? Of betting? What are the duties of parents with respect to their children, in view of the solemn vow made when these children were baptized? Is this vow less than an oath?

REFERENCES
1) GROSHEIDE, *Mattheus*, p. 64.
2) p. 146. The oath of the Boy Scouts is given, e. g., on p. 33 of *Boy Scouts of America*, 32nd edition.

READING AND STUDY HELPS
Besides the commentaries previously referred to, see W. Geesink, *Geref. Ethiek* II, pp. 302-306. Art. "Oath" in *I. S. B. E.* A very excellent article on "Eed" in the *Chr. Enc.* Dr. T. P. Kaiser, op. cit., pp. 87-98. C. A. Blanchard, *Modern Secret Societies*, esp. pp. 101, 102. The *How Book of Scouting and Boy Scouts of America*, published by the Boy Scouts of America, 200 Fifth Ave., N. Y. Works on H. Catechism, Question and Answer 101. Works on the Third Commandment. See previous Outline. Esp. *E Voto* III, pp. 608-615. Art. "Kwakers" in *Chr. Enc.* Art. "Friends, Society of," in *Enc. Brit.*, and in the *New Standard Enc.*

CHAPTER XI

THE RIGHTEOUSNESS OF THE KINGDOM
(VERSUS THE TRADITIONAL JEWISH INTERPRETATION OF THE LAW)

The Law of Retaliation

MATTHEW 5:38-42.
> "Ye have heard that it was said, An eye for an eye, and a tooth for a tooth: but I say unto you, Resist not him that is evil: but whosoever smiteth thee on thy right cheek, turn to him the other also. And if any man would go to law with thee, and take away thy coat, let him have thy cloak also. And whosoever shall compel thee to go one mile, go with him two. Give to him that asketh thee, and from him that would borrow of thee turn not thou away."

I. THE PHARISAIC INTERPRETATION OF THE LAW OF RETALIATION.

A. "YE HAVE HEARD THAT IT WAS SAID, AN EYE FOR AN EYE, AND A TOOTH FOR A TOOTH . . . ."

These words are taken from the O. T. In Ex. 21:24, 25 we read, ". . . . eye for eye, tooth for tooth, hand for hand, foot for foot, burning for burning, wound for wound, stripe for stripe." Cf. Lev. 24:20 and Deut. 19:21. This was a law for the government in order that the practice of seeking private and personal revenge might be discouraged. The O. T. passages do not mean, "Take personal revenge whenever you are wronged." They mean just the opposite, namely, "Do not take private and personal revenge, but let justice be administered *publicly* according to the law of retaliation." That this commandment relates indeed to the public administration of criminal law is very plain from the context in which it occurs, e. g., Lev. 24:14, "Bring forth him that hath cursed without the camp; and let all that heard him lay their hands upon his head, and let all the congregation stone him."

The Pharisees, however, used this law in order to justify personal retribution and revenge; hence, they quoted these O. T. words with the intention of defeating their very purpose. Hence, also with respect to this law their tradition had as its purpose: to render the law of God of no effect. Even the O. T. very clearly forbids personal revenge, Lev. 19:18, "Thou shalt not take vengeance, nor bear any grudge against the children of thy people; but thou shalt love thy neighbor as thyself: I am Jehovah." Cf. Prov. 20:22, "Say not thou, I will recompense evil: Wait for Jehovah, and he will save thee." Prov. 24:29, "Say not, I will do so to him as he hath done to me; I will render to the man according to his work."

B. IT IS INTERESTING TO NOTE THAT THE ERROR OF THE PHARISEES, NAMELY, CONFUSING THE *PUBLIC* ADMINISTRATION OF JUSTICE WITH THE DUTIES OF THE INDIVIDUAL, STILL EXISTS. Just as the Pharisees used the O. T. law regarding retaliation in order that they might justify personal revenge, so the ultra-pacifists of today use the words of Jesus, found in verses 39 to 42—words which plainly have reference to *personal* forbearance —in order to attack the public administration by the magistrate. Fundamentally, the Pharisaic interpretation of the law of retaliation and the Pacifist interpretation of the words of Jesus result from the same confusion of concepts.

II. CHRIST'S RESTRICTION OF THE LAW OF RETALIATION TO THE SPHERE OF THE STATE, BY PREACHING THE GOSPEL OF FORBEARANCE AND LOVE FOR THE SPHERE OF THE KINGDOM.

A. ". . . . But I say unto you, Resist not him that is evil . . . ."

1. Many have interpreted these words as a condemnation of all wars. This is the view of Tolstoy, of most Anabaptists, Mennonites, Quakers and ultra-pacifists. But is this view correct? This brings us to the question:

2. Does this passage, "Resist not him that is evil," make it unconditionally wrong for a person to go to war? We answer, "It does not," for:

(*a*) It is very evident from the entire context (see esp. verse 40 and verse 42) that Jesus is speaking about proper relations between *persons;* he is not speaking about governments. This passage is clear enough providing one examines the context.

(*b*) During the O. T. Dispensation God commanded the Israelites to exterminate the Canaanites in order to *punish* them for their great wickedness, and in order to show *mercy* to Israel and to the whole world. "If the sins of these people had not received the rebuke which they merited, they would have polluted the chosen people of God out of whom the Messiah was to come forth."[1] Cf. Ps. 126:17, "To him that smote great kings; for his *lovingkindness* endureth forever." It may be argued, however, that today God does not issue direct commandments whereby he orders a nation to go to war, and that, therefore, this argument derived from the O. T. does not hold at all. However, if war is as such wrong, would the holy God ever have ordered any nation to make use of this instrument?

(c) God not only directly commanded war but he also approved of David's desire to resort to arms as a defensive measure, I Sam. 23:1, 2.

(d) Scripture everywhere proclaims the right of self-defense. Cf. Ex. 22:2; Deut. 19; Acts 21:27 ff., etc. "When a nation takes up weapons in self-defense for the sole purpose of restraining unlawful aggression, it is not sinning. The sin lies with those who because of pride, the desire for conquest, and the ambition to be great make an unlawful aggression upon an unselfish, law-abiding and peaceful community."[2]

QUESTIONS FOR DISCUSSION. What is the line of demarcation between an aggresive and a defensive war? Was the recent war between China and Japan an act of aggression on the part of Japan or merely a defensive measure? Cff. the Lytton Report in *Current History Magazine*, November, 1932.

(e) From Gen. 9 and Rom. 13 it follows that a nation has a right to defend itself against an aggressor. "If a government has a legitimate power of the sword to protect its good citizens against its evil ones, it also has the right and the duty to protect the whole nation from wanton aggression and attack of another nation."[3]

(f) John the Baptist did not demand that the soldiers should forsake their military calling, Lk. 3:14; Jesus praised the centurion and healed his servant; he did not demand of the centurion that he forsake his profession, Matt. 8:5-13. Cf. also Acts 10 in regard to Cornelius, the centurion.

(g) Nevertheless, the Christian does not glory in war. On the contrary, he will do everything in his power to prevent wars and to remove the *causes* of war. Cf. Ps. 46:9; 68:30c; Is. 2:4.

QUESTION FOR DISCUSSION. To what degree should the Christian support existing measures and instruments against war?

3. We have pointed out that according to the context the passage under discussion has to do with proper relations between the citizens of the kingdom of God. Should this passage be taken literally? Answer: No, in view of the succeeding verses it should not be taken literally, but has this meaning: "Resist not evil with *vengeance*, i. e., with measures which arise from an unforgiving, unrelenting, grudgeful spirit." If Jesus meant to condemn every form of resistance to evil, then even the preaching of the Word, nay even Christian character and example would be forbidden!

B. ". . . . But whosoever smiteth thee on thy right cheek, turn to him the other also. And if any man would go to law with thee, and take away thy coat, let him have thy cloak also. . . Give to him that asketh thee."

1. The words in regard to "turning the other cheek" are not to be taken literally, for Jesus himself did not carry them out literally, John 18:22. Meaning: "Rather suffer wrong twice, than do wrong once."

QUESTION FOR DISCUSSION. Does this mean that a Christian may never insist upon his rights?

If we keep in mind continually that Jesus in these words forbids *revenge, a vindictive and unforgiving spirit,* we shall have no difficulty. To "turn the other cheek" means to show plainly by our very deeds, words, and attitude that we are not possessed with a spirit of rancor but instead with a spirit of love. Rom. 12:19-21 offers an excellent commentary on these words of Jesus.

2. "And if any man would go to law with thee," etc. Meaning:

(*a*) Implication: you yourself must not start the law-suit against a brother.

(*b*) When anyone would rob you of earthly possessions, it is far better to be defrauded than to do wrong. Cf. Heb. 10:34; I Cor. 6:7, 8. Do not return evil for evil. "Avenge not yourselves." If any man threatens you with a lawsuit to take away your coat, i. e., the tunic worn next to the body, do not resentfully contest this lawsuit, but rather than doing that, let him also have your outer robe, a robe considered so indispensable that the law required that when taken as a pledge it had to be returned "before the sun goeth down," Ex. 22:26, 27, since it served as a cover during sleep, Deut. 24:12, 13.

3. "Whosoever shall compel thee to go one mile, go with him two." This statement has reference to the postal service. Postal couriers were permitted to demand the services of individuals and their animals in order that their trip might not be delayed. Now Jesus means to say, "If any one of you is compelled to travel one Roman mile, 1680 yards, even if he be pressed into service unjustly, it will be better by far to travel an extra mile of his own accord than to reveal a spirit of rebellion." Again the same lesson: Instead of manifesting a spirit of revenge, as the Pharisees would have you do, show the greatest degree of good-will and generosity.

4. "Give to him that asketh thee, and from him that would borrow of thee turn not thou away." Meaning: when your brother is in distress, and asks you for help, then do not turn a deaf ear to him. Rather, give; even though he has previously wronged you. Summary: the law of retaliation is not to be practiced in the kingdom of heaven!

REFERENCES
1) Dr. J. H. Bruinooge, *Banner* of Nov. 8, 1929.
2) Dr. J. H. Bruinooge, *Banner* of Feb. 7, 1930.
3) Dr. C. Bouma, *Federation Messenger* of Feb., 1932.

READING AND STUDY HELPS

We refer you especially to three very splendid articles: Dr. J. H. Bruinooge, art. *Is War Lawful?* in *Banners* of Nov. 8 and Nov. 15, 1929 (see also *Banner* of Feb. 7, 1930); Dr. C. Bouma, art. *The Christian and Going to War*, in the *Fed. Messenger* of Feb., 1932; and Mr. G. M. Den Hartogh, art "Oorlog" in *Chr. Enc.* Further: W. Geesink, *Geref. Ethiek* II, p. 418. J. Stalker, *The Ethic of Jesus*, chap. 16. G. M. Den Hartogh, art. "Vergelding" in *Chr. Enc.* Art. "War" in Hasting's *Encyclopedia of Rel. and Ethics.* Dr. T. P. Kaiser, op. cit., pp. 101-114. Be sure to read that excellent booklet by Prof. A. Pieters *The Christian Attitude Toward War.* The views of extreme pacifists are found in C. M. Sheldon's *He Is Here*, Kirby Page's *Jesus or Christianity*, Sherwood Eddy's *A World Mind*, cf. Dr. F. W. Norwood's *The Supreme Task of This Age*, and Dr. E. F. Tittle's *War and Human Nature.* The last three are articles in *Voices of the Age.* Cf. also the pacifist journals: *The Christian Century*, and *The World Tomorrow.*

CHAPTER XII

THE RIGHTEOUSNESS OF THE KINGDOM
(VERSUS THE TRADITIONAL JEWISH INTERPRETATION OF THE LAW)

Love Toward the Neighbor

MATTHEW 5:43-48.

> "Ye have heard that it was said, Thou shalt love thy neighbor, and hate thine enemy: but I say unto you, Love your enemies, and pray for them that persecute you; that ye may be sons of your Father who is in heaven: for he maketh his sun to rise on the evil and the good, and sendeth rain on the just and the unjust. For if ye love them that love you, what reward have ye? do not even the publicans the same? And if ye salute your brethren only, what do ye more than others? do not even the Gentiles the same? Ye therefore shall be perfect, as your heavenly Father is perfect."

I. THE PHARISAIC INTERPRETATION OF THE LAW OF LOVE TOWARD THE NEIGHBOR.

"YE HAVE HEARD THAT IT WAS SAID, THOU SHALT LOVE THY NEIGHBOR, AND HATE THINE ENEMY." The contrast between the Pharisaic interpretation of the law and Christ's interpretation is nowhere as striking and as flagrant as at this point. The command, "Thou shalt love thy neighbor," occurs more than once in the Law. Cf. Lev. 19:18, "Thou shalt not take vengeance, nor bear any grudge against the children of thy people; but thou shalt love thy neighbor as thyself: I am Jehovah." Cf. Ex. 23:4 and 5; Prov. 25:21, 22, etc. Now, according to Jesus my "neighbor" is any one, without exception, with whom I come into contact, any one who needs my assistance in any way. Even my enemy (i. e., the one who hates me) is my neighbor. I must show him kindness. Cf. Luke 10: the parable of the Good Samaritan. Christ very emphatically teaches in that parable that it is wrong for us to divide mankind into two halves: enemies and friends. Instead of asking, "Who is my neighbor?" one should "prove himself neighbor" unto everyone, Lk. 10:36, 37. The O. T. teaches the same lesson, essentially. Cf. Prov. 24:17, 29; 25:21, 22; Ps. 7:5; Job 31:29. Furthermore, compare the noble example of Joseph, Gen. 45:1; of David, I Sam. 24:7; 24:5; and of Elisha, II Kings 6:22.

Now over against this view which is prominent in both Testaments, but especially in the New, the Pharisees divided mankind into two groups: neighbors and enemies, and taught that one should love the former and hate the latter. The words, ". . . . and hate thine enemy," are found nowhere in the O. T. Cf. Ex. 12:43-49. By adding these words to the law of God the Pharisees made the commandment of no effect. Moreover, the Pharisees further mutilated the law of God by purposely omitting the words "as thyself." (Cf. for exceptions Mk. 12:33; Lk. 10:27.) Whereas the purpose of the O. T. law was to indicate how much one should love, they, by omitting "as thyself," made it appear as if the real aim of the law was to show *whom* we should love and whom we should hate.

QUESTION FOR DISCUSSION. But, if even the Old Testament teaches love toward those who hate us, how do you explain the so-called imprecatory psalms? Cf. Pss. 5, 35, 55, 59, 69, 79, 109, 129, 58, 83, 137.

II. CHRIST'S INTERPRETATION OF THIS LAW OF LOVE.

A. Christ's interpretation as such: ". . . BUT I SAY UNTO YOU, LOVE YOUR ENEMIES (bless them that curse you, do good to them that hate you— A. V.) AND PRAY FOR THEM THAT (despitefully use you and—A. V.) PERSECUTE YOU." It is not very easy to determine whether the Authorized or the Revised Version should be followed here. If we follow the A. V., then we notice the beauty and completeness of the precept: love in *thought*, namely, "Love your enemies;" then, love in *word*, namely, "Bless them that curse you;" love in *act*, namely, "Do good to them that hate you;" and love shown in *intercession*, "Pray for them that . . . persecute you." The word for "enemy" means "personal enemy," i. e., the one who hates you. Jesus says, as it were, "Also that enemy is your neighbor; hence, you should love him." Christ has himself given the example, Lk. 23:34. Moreover, Christ uses a very strong word for *love* here. See *Christ's Parting Words,* Outlines VI-A and VIII, *Federation Messenger,* October, 1933. He does not speak of a merely natural affection but he demands a higher love: a love for the sake of principle, a love that has for its object those who are not lovable in themselves as well as the others. Says Lenski, "I cannot like a filthy, vicious beggar and make him my personal friend; I cannot like a low, mean criminal, who may have robbed me and threatened my life; I cannot like a false, lying, slanderous fellow, who perhaps has vilified me again and again—but I can, by the grace of Jesus Christ, love them all, see what is wrong with them, desire and work to do them only good, most of all to free them from their vicious ways."[1] Moreover, according to the original Jesus says: "*Keep on loving* your enemies, . . . continue to pray for them, even though they continue to persecute you."

QUESTIONS FOR DISCUSSION. What must we think of expressions like "I'll get even with him," used at times even by members of the church? Jesus teaches us to love even our enemies. Does this mean that we should love enemies and Christian brethren *equally?* In this connection: in the distribution of our gifts, should we give as much to funds that aim to promote civic welfare, e. g., the community chest, as to the Christian Psychopathic Hospitals and Sanatoriums, i. e., to strictly Christian institutions of mercy? Does Scripture give any rule to guide us in the proper distribution of our gifts?

B. The Purpose of loving one's enemies. This purpose is in reality one. For the sake of convenience we may differentiate as follows:

1. "*. . . . That ye may be sons of your Father who is in heaven:* for he maketh his sun to rise on the evil and the good, and sendeth rain on the just and the unjust."

Jesus does not mean that by loving one's enemies one will gradually become a son of the Heavenly Father; but that by so doing one will become transformed into the image of the Father, and will begin to resemble the Father, as sons should do. Sunshine and rain were considered very great blessings, especially in the Orient. Jesus here teaches us not only *that* the Father in heaven sends rain and sunshine upon believers and unbelievers alike, but also *why* he does it, namely, motivated by love toward all. This is very evident from Lk. 6:35, 36, "But love your enemies, and do them good . . . and ye shall be sons of the Most High: *for he is kind toward the unthankful and evil. Be ye merciful even as your Father is merciful.*" The argument, therefore, is very plainly this: "You must show kindness not only to believers, but also to unbelievers, for your Heavenly Father does the same."[1]

QUESTIONS FOR DISCUSSION. Does not this passage clearly teach common grace?[2] What do you understand by common grace? Is there a danger, however, of over-emphasizing this doctrine? Does common grace furnish us with a principle of co-operation between the Christian and the man of the world in all spheres except the strictly religious sphere? Does it really? What are the "Three Points" laid down by the 1924 Synod of the Christian Reformed Church?

2. *That you may differ from the world:* ". . . FOR IF YE LOVE THEM THAT LOVE YOU, WHAT REWARD HAVE YE? DO NOT EVEN THE PUBLICANS THE SAME? AND IF YE SALUTE YOUR BRETHREN ONLY, WHAT DO YE MORE THAN OTHERS? DO NOT EVEN THE GENTILES THE SAME?"

Jesus hereby clearly indicates that the morality of the Pharisees is not any higher in this respect than the morality of the publicans: Jews who were hated because they collected the taxes for an alien and tyrannical power and were generally notorious for their dishonest exactions. Even these publicans loved their friends, and this was all that was required according to the Pharisaic interpretation of the Law. Even Gentiles practiced this kind of love. Jesus emphasizes the need of Christian distinctiveness: the Pharisee, publican, and Gentile loved and saluted those who loved them; Christ tells us to love even those who hate us. ".... what reward have ye?"

QUESTION FOR DISCUSSION. But, should the Christian ever do anything with a view to receiving a reward?

3. *That you may be perfect:* "YE THEREFORE SHALL BE PERFECT, AS YOUR HEAVENLY FATHER IS PERFECT." The original word which has been translated "perfect" means "brought to completion, full-grown, lacking nothing." A love which has for its object only one's *friends* and does not embrace one's *enemies* as well is *incomplete*. It has not reached the *goal*. It is not *perfect*. Because of the previous context it is probable that Christ had reference especially to perfection in *love*. Because our Father is perfect, we, as sons, should be perfect also. Cf. Lev. 11:44; 20:7, 26; Deut. 18:13; Lev. 19:2; Eph. 5:1; and I Peter 1:15, 16.

REFERENCES

[1] LENSKI, *Interpretation of Matthew*, p. 240.

[2] Cf. L. BERKHOF, *De Drie Punten in Alle Deelen Gereformeerd*, pp. 26, 27.

READING AND STUDY HELPS

On the question of common grace see L. Berkhof, *De Drie Punten in Alle Deelen Gereformeerd;* Dr. H. Bavinck, *De Algemeene Genade;* A. Kuyper, *De Gemeene Gratie;* V. Hepp, *Het Misverstand;* J. K. Van Baalen, *De Loochening der Gem. Gratie.* The other side: H. Hoeksema and H. Danhof, *Van Zonde en Genade; Niet Doopersch maar Gereformeerd,* etc., etc. English: M. J. Bosma, *Exp. of Ref. Doctrine,* pp. 32, 33; R. B. Kuiper, *As to Being Reformed,* pp. 109 ff., etc., etc. Besides commentaries already mentioned, see Dr. T. P. Kaiser, op. cit., pp. 117-129. On imprecatory Psalms see *I. S. B. E.*, vol. IV, p. 2494. Art. "Vloekpsalmen" in *Chr. Enc.*

CHAPTER XIII

THE RIGHTEOUSNESS OF THE KINGDOM
Its Essence With Respect to Our Relation to God:

The Secret Devotion of the Heart, Illustrated with Respect to Almsgiving

MATTHEW 6:1-4.

"Take heed that ye do not your righteousness before men, to be seen of them: else ye have no reward with your Father who is in heaven. When therefore thou doest alms, sound not the trumpet before thee, as the hypocrites do in the synagogues and in the streets, that they may have glory of men. Verily I say unto you, They have received their reward. But when thou doest alms, let not thy left hand know what thy right hand doeth: that thine alms may be in secret: and thy Father who seeth in secret shall recompense thee."

I. CONNECTION.

At this point it is well for us to glance back for a moment in order that we may see just how the new paragraph of the sermon is related to the rest. In Matthew 5:1-16 Jesus described the *citizens* of the kingdom: their character and blessedness, and their relation to the world. They are to be the salt of the earth and the light of the world. In Matt. 5:17 Jesus begins to discuss the *righteousness* of the kingdom: the ethical ideal in accordance with which the citizens should pattern their thoughts, words, and deeds. When we read the very first verse discussed in *this* chapter, we notice that Christ is still teaching us concerning the righteousness of the kingdom. We learned:

1. That this righteousness is in complete harmony with the Law, Matt. 5:17-19. Jesus did not come to destroy but to fulfil the law.

2. That this righteousness is not in harmony with the righteousness of scribes and Pharisees, Matt. 5:20-48. This point was illustrated with respect to:

(*a*) The sixth commandment. Scribes and Pharisees viewed as transgression of this commandment only such acts as were punishable in court. Jesus calls anger against the brother murder.

(*b*) The seventh commandment. Scribes and Pharisees narrowed down this precept so that only literal adultery was forbidden. According to Christ's interpretation it forbids adultery in the heart.

(*c*) The commandment concerning the oath. According to scribes and Pharisees only those were guilty of transgressing this commandment who failed to keep their oaths which they had sworn by literally taking the name of God on their lips. Christ teaches that all thoughtless oaths dishonor God.

(*d*) The commandment concerning the law of retaliation. The Jewish leaders taught that this law should be applied to the attitude of one person toward another. Christ pointed out that this law should be limited to the public administration of justice, and that the members of the kingdom should be guided in their relation to one another by love and forbearance, never by retaliation nor by the spirit of revenge.

(*e*) The commandment concerning love toward the neighbor. The scribes and Pharisees restricted the meaning of the word "neighbor," and taught that one should love the neighbor and hate the enemy. Jesus countered this by teaching that all men are our neighbors and that, consequently, we should love even our enemies.

Having seen, therefore, that the righteousness of the kingdom *is not in harmony with that of scribes and Pharisees*, it is but natural for us to ask: Then what *is* the character or essence of the righteousness of the kingdom? In answer to this question we learn first of all that it consists in loving God above all, and therefore in: *the secret devotion of the heart to God*, rather than the merely outward display of good works "to be seen of men." This point is illustrated first of all with respect to almsgiving.

II. STATEMENT OF THE UNDERLYING PRINCIPLE WHICH SHOULD CONTROL OUR ACTIONS:

"TAKE HEED THAT YE DO NOT YOUR RIGHTEOUSNESS BEFORE (in front of) MEN, TO BE SEEN OF THEM: ELSE YE HAVE NO REWARD WITH YOUR FATHER WHO IS IN HEAVEN."

1. Notice that whereas up to this point Christ has condemned the *teaching* of the scribes and

Pharisees, he now begins to condemn their *acts*, their *practice*.

2. Meaning, in general: when we try to keep the law (for righteousness is conformity to the law) in order to be seen of men, i. e., with a selfish aim, then we have no reward. Hence, we should strive to keep the law out of *gratitude* or *love*. Jesus says, as it were, by doing your so-called good works you are either aiming at your own glory or at the glory of the Father in heaven. If the former is true, then that honor which you receive from men is itself your reward, your only reward. You will not receive the heavenly reward in addition by and by. If, however, motivated by love you seek to promote the glory of the Father in heaven, then you will receive a great reward in the hereafter. This reward is, of course, of grace. God sees the heart. He knows whether or not it is really devoted to him and to his service: the essence of true righteousness.

III. THIS UNDERLYING PRINCIPLE APPLIED TO ALMSGIVING.

A. *The practice of the Pharisees:* "WHEN THEREFORE THOU DOEST ALMS, SOUND NOT THE TRUMPET BEFORE THEE, AS THE HYPOCRITES DO IN THE SYNAGOGUES AND IN THE STREETS, THAT THEY MAY HAVE GLORY OF MEN. VERILY I SAY UNTO YOU, THEY HAVE RECEIVED THEIR REWARD."

1. Did the Pharisees actually "sound the trumpet" when they were about to give alms? Cyril of Alexandria states that it was a Jewish

custom to summon the poor by trumpet to receive alms, much as hogs on the farms are called by the farmer to the trough.[1]) In view of the fact, however, that synagogues are mentioned, and it is not very likely that they would literally sound these trumpets for this purpose in the house of worship, and also in view of the fact that Christ makes much use of symbolical language in this sermon, it is more likely that Christ referred to the fact that the Pharisees did everything in their power to advertise their gifts.[2])

2. The Pharisees were called "hypocrites" because while they *pretended* to *give,* they really *intended* to *receive,* namely, honor from men.

3. "They have received their reward." The real meaning is: "They can sign the receipt of their reward. And that receipt is marked: *Received in full.*" When you receive your winter coal supply, you are asked to sign a receipt, stating that you have received it. Says Christ, "The Pharisees can also sign a receipt." No future reward awaits them.[3])

B. *The practice as enjoined by Christ:* "BUT WHEN THOU DOEST ALMS, LET NOT THY LEFT HAND KNOW WHAT THY RIGHT HAND DOETH: THAT THINE ALMS MAY BE IN SECRET: AND THY FATHER WHO SEETH IN SECRET SHALL RECOMPENSE THEE."

1. The expression, "Let not thy left hand know," etc., is, of course, a figure. Meaning: your giving must be motivated by true love toward the poor; hence, you must not seek publicity.

QUESTIONS FOR DISCUSSION. Must we conclude from this that we may never sign our name when we make a pledge? These words of Jesus have been applied by some as an argument against the budget to pay congregational expenses. Show that such reasoning is wrong. Should gifts for charitable institutions or enterprises be acknowledged in the church-papers?

2. Even though *men* do not see your gift, nevertheless *God* does see it, for he sees in secret, i. e., your secret acts as well as your public deeds. The "reward" consists of peace of conscience here, i. e., a consciousness of the fact that God approves of your deed, and glory in the hereafter.

REFERENCES
1) A. T. ROBERTSON, *The Pharisees and Jesus*, p. 134.
2) GROSHEIDE, *Mattheus*, p. 70.
3) A. DEISSMANN, *Light from the Ancient East*, p. 119. Same author, *The N. T. in the Light of Modern Research*, pp. 86, 87.

READING AND STUDY HELPS
Commentaries on Matthew and on the Sermon on the Mount (see Outline I). Dr. T. P. Kaiser, op. cit., pp. 133-146; A. T. Robertson, *The Pharisees and Jesus*, p. 133 ff.; Dr. W. Geesink, *Geref. Ethiek* II, pp. 205, 334, 371; J. Stalker, *The Ethic of Jesus*, pp. 68, 72-74, 138, 302, 321.

CHAPTER XIV

THE RIGHTEOUSNESS OF THE KINGDOM
Its Essence With Respect to Our Relation to God:

The Secret Devotion of the Heart, Illustrated with Respect to Prayer

MATTHEW 6:5-8.

"And when ye pray, ye shall not be as the hypocrites: for they love to stand and pray in the synagogues and in the corners of the streets, that they may be seen of men. Verily I say unto you, They have received their reward. But thou, when thou prayest, enter into thine inner chamber, and having shut thy door, pray to thy Father who is in secret, and thy Father who seeth in secret shall recompense thee. And in praying use not vain repetitions, as the Gentiles do: for they think that they shall be heard for their much speaking. Be not therefore like unto them: for your Father knoweth what things ye have need of, before ye ask him."

In order to get this lesson clearly before our minds, we shall discuss the verses in the following order: verse 5 (the prayer of the hypocrite); verse 7 (the vain repetitions of the Gentile); verses 6 and 8 (the secret devotion of the citizen of the kingdom).

I. THE PRAYER OF THE HYPOCRITE.

A. The Nature of this Prayer. It is a prayer of the lips and not of the heart. ". . . they (the hypocrites) love to stand and pray in the synagogues, and in the corners of the streets . . ."

1. *Hypocrites.* A most cutting word of reproach. Jesus uses it about twenty-five times. He had a right to use it because he knew the *hearts* of men. *We* do not. "Let no man, unless he is sure of the insight of Christ, and the Spirit of Christ, accuse his fellow man of hypocrisy."[1)] Generally speaking—experience teaches us that we must leave room for exceptions—it is a good rule to examine one's own motives thoroughly, but to assume that the motives of the brother or sister in the Lord are pure. The word hypocrisy originally meant stage-playing, acting a part in a play. The actor in a play is never *himself;* he always *pretends* to be some other person. Hence, the term "hypocrite" soon received the meaning: a pretender; one who in actual life "assumes a character other than the real, with the design of gaining commendation." These hypocrites *pretended* to be giving glory to God by means of prayer, while they *intended* to gain glory for themselves.

2. These hypocrites (scribes and Pharisees, Matt. 5:20) would take care that at the appointed time for prayer they happened to be "in the synagogues or in the corners of the streets," i. e., in those places where they would be seen by every one. Notice especially the word "corners of the streets," really: the corners of the *public squares,* where a multitude of people was always present.

3. Many have interpreted these words of Jesus as if they implied a condemnation of *pub-*

lic prayer, e. g., the prayer of the minister in church. That, however, is missing the point entirely. Jesus does not refer to public prayer, but he condemns *personal prayer in public places,* i. e., prayer in which no one else was expected to join. A minister "leads" ("gaat voor") in prayer. He is the "voice" of the congregation. Pharisees and scribes offered their personal prayers in a public place. Moreover, even a personal prayer in a public place *may* at times be perfectly proper, but it is to be wholly condemned when

B. THE PURPOSE OF THIS PRAYER (is) to be seen of men. The righteousness of the scribes and Pharisees was ostentatious. They wanted to "show off," to "shine."

QUESTIONS FOR DISCUSSIONS. At a meeting which I attended some time ago a missionary asked each person in the audience to tell how many minutes he spent in prayer every day. In view of the words of Jesus which we are discussing what was wrong with such a request? Should we have prayer-meetings in our churches; meetings in which every one who so desires is permitted to lead in prayer? Where lies the danger, or is there no danger?

C. THE RESULT OF THIS PRAYER. "Verily, I say unto you, They have received their reward." For the meaning of these words see Chapter XIII.

II. THE PRAYER OF THE GENTILE.

A. THE NATURE OF THIS PRAYER. It consists of "vain repetitions." "And in praying use not vain repetitions as the Gentiles do. . . . ."

Cf. the prayer of the priests of Baal, I Kings 18:26. Also: the Pater Nosters assigned to

Roman Catholics. Also: the prayer wheels of the Buddhists.

QUESTIONS FOR DISCUSSION. Is it not true that prayers at meals are apt to deteriorate into "vain repetitions"? Should these prayers be lengthy? Just what constitutes the real "family altar"? Why is it so very important?

B. THE PURPOSE OF THIS PRAYER. "For they think that they shall be heard for their much speaking." Heathens viewed their gods as angry beings who needed to be *placated*, i. e., to be brought from a state of hostile feeling to one of friendliness; from ill-disposed to well-disposed. Hence, they would bring sacrifices, as gifts to the gods in order to *appease* them. Hence, also, they would offer their "vain repetitions." Jesus means: in this respect the scribes and Pharisees have become like unto the heathen: *"much speaking"* characterizes the prayer of both. Neither the hypocrite nor the heathen gives his *heart* to God. *That* is the point. The righteousness of the kingdom consists in this: *the secret devotion of the heart!*

III. THE PRAYER OF THE CITIZEN OF THE KINGDOM.

"And when ye pray, ye shall not be as the hypocrites . . . But thou, when thou prayest, enter into thine inner chamber, and having shut thy door, pray to thy Father who is in secret, and thy Father who seeth in secret shall recompense thee. . . . Be not, therefore, like unto them (the heathen), for your Father knoweth what things ye have need of, before ye ask him."

A. THE NATURE OF THIS PRAYER:

1. It consists of the *secret devotion of the heart*. The scribes and Pharisees wanted to gain the *eye* of *men;* Christians seek to gain the *ear* of *God*. Hence, in prayer, the soul of God's child comes into contact with the soul of God. Prayer is the sacred and reverent conversation of the soul with God. Prayer means to draw near unto God. Says Dr. A. Kuyper, Sr., "To be near unto God means such nearness to God as to see him with the eyes, to be aware of his presence in the heart, to hear him with the ear, and to have every barrier removed that thus far kept him aloof. To be near unto God means to be near him in one of two ways: *either to feel as though we were caught up into heaven, or as though God had come down to us in our loneliness, sorrow, or joy.*"[2] Notice the *singular*: Jesus does not say, "But *ye* when *ye* pray." He says, "But *thou,* when *thou* prayest." The "inner chamber," i. e., one's "own room," at times on the roof: a special room for prayer and meditation. "Shut thy door" to keep others out. Notice the contrast between this and the practice of scribes and Pharisees, between *secret devotion* and *public display*. This secret devotion of the citizen of the kingdom has for its purpose the glory of God; hence, it is much broader in its scope than the prayer of the hypocrite and of the heathen. It may consist of: (a) *confession of sin;* (b) *consultation:* asking for guidance; (c) *supplication;* (d) *intercession;* (e) *gratulation;* (f) *adoration;* (g) *dedication.* In

a good prayer several of these elements are combined.

QUESTIONS FOR DISCUSSION. Just what is meant by each of these elements? Which do you consider the most important?

The emphasis of the contrast which Jesus draws must be carefully observed. *Literally* considered, the point of the contrast is this: our prayers should be *secret* instead of *public*. Yet, that is not the *real* point. The *real* point is this: our prayers should be *sincere* instead of *insincere*, as were the prayers of the scribes and Pharisees.

2. It arises from and is motivated by *trust in God as our Father*. Read carefully verses 6 and 8. Notice that over against both the "hypocrites" and the "heathen" Christ emphasizes that true prayer is a prayer to "the *Father*." To the heathen God was not a *Father;* neither was this Father-relation emphasized by scribes and Pharisees. In the teaching of Jesus it is central. The words, "thy Father who seeth in secret," have been explained in the previous Chapter. A father understands his child. Hence, the child does not need to say very much with respect to its needs. The Father in heaven is omniscient. He "knoweth what things ye have need of." Hence, vain repetitions are out of place in addressing him.

QUESTION FOR DISCUSSION. Is God the Father of all men?

B. THE RESULT OF THIS PRAYER. "Thy Father .... shall recompense thee." See I John 5:14. The point is: the Pharisees have received their reward from men; the Christian receives and will receive his reward from the Father. True prayer will certainly be answered. EVERY TRUE PRAYER IS HEARD. There are, however, prayers which do not ring true; which are not heard, therefore. Ps. 66:18, "If I regard iniquity in my heart, *the Lord will not hear me."* Notice the following hindrances to prayer:

(1) refusing to fight against a certain sinful habit, Ps. 66:18; Is. 59:1, 2;

(2) praying with a selfish purpose, Jas. 4:3;

(3) having "idols in the heart," Ezek. 14:3;

(4) maintaining a wrong attitude toward one's husband or wife, I Pet. 3:7;

(5) harboring a grudge, Matt. 6:14, 15;

(6) "stopping one's ears to the cry of the poor," Prov. 21:13;

(7) doubting whether God will answer, Jas. 1:5-7.

REFERENCES
1) C. B. McAffee, *Studies in the Sermon on the Mount*, p. 92.

2) A. Kuyper, Sr., *To Be Near Unto God*, first meditation.

READING AND STUDY HELPS
The book *To Be Near Unto God* by A. Kuyper, Sr. (original: *Nabij God te Zijn*) should be in every home. And, of course, you all have — at least *should* have — *The Incense of Prayer* by Rev. B. H. Spalink. Cf. further, A. T. Robertson, *Concerning God the Father;* art. "Hypocrisy," "Hypocrite," in *I. S. B. E.;* R. E. Golladay's *Sermons on the Catechism*, vol. III, "The Lord's Prayer," is very good. See also Ds. F. C. Meyster, art. "Bidden," in *Chr. Enc.* Further: commentaries, etc., mentioned in the First Outline.

CHAPTER XV

THE RIGHTEOUSNESS OF THE KINGDOM
Its Essence With Respect to Our Relation to God:

The Secret Devotion of the Heart, Illustrated with Respect to the Lord's Prayer

MATTHEW 6:9a.
"After this manner therefore pray ye: Our Father who art in heaven."

I. PROBLEMS IN PRAYER LIFE.

A. THE PROBLEM WHICH PRESENTS ITSELF WHEN ONE CONSIDERS THE CONNECTION BETWEEN VERSES 8 AND 9. That problem, briefly stated, is this: "If God knows all things, then why should we tell him our needs?" Be sure to take note of the strange and altogether unexpected train of thought here. Jesus has just warned his hearers against the use of vain repetitions, "as the Gentiles do." He continued by saying, "Be not therefore like unto them: *for your Father knoweth what things ye have need of before ye ask him.*" We naturally expect the next sentence to be, "Hence, whereas your Father knows your needs, you should not pray at all." But, instead of this, the Lord says the exact opposite, namely, "seeing that your Father knoweth what things ye have need of, before ye ask him; *therefore*, after this manner *pray ye*." In answer to this difficulty, notice the following:

(1) The real point of contrast which Jesus is making here is between the *fear and distrust* which characterizes the prayer of the heathen; hence, his vain repetitions (he does not believe *one* prayer will be sufficient to *placate* his god) on the one hand, and the *trust or confidence* which should be the distinctive mark of the Christian's prayer, on the other. The sense, then, is this: "Because you have a *Father* who *loves* you and *understands* your needs; hence, the attitude of *trust* should characterize your prayer, i. e., you should call God your *Father*, and pray *after this manner*, viz., Our *Father*," etc.

(2) *Just because* the mother *understands* the child so thoroughly and *knows* its needs far better than any stranger, the little one will go to mother rather than to any one else. Similarly, *just because our Father understands our needs so thoroughly, we should go to him instead of relying on the help of man.*

B. OTHER PROBLEMS IN PRAYER LIFE:

QUESTIONS FOR DISCUSSION. Is it not foolish to pray for rain? A potter prayed that it might not rain, so that his pottery might dry; his brother, who was a gardener and lived in the same locality, prayed for rain upon his plants. Is it reasonable to suppose that God can answer such conflicting prayers? Is it not foolish, then, to pray for rain? Another problem: there are modernists who believe that prayer has subjective value only: it makes you feel better; in *that* sense it helps; but God does not actually *hear* that prayer; there are others, however, cf. e. g., the book, *Meeting the Challenge of Modern Doubt*, who reason that prayer is more than a "psychological device to bolster up your self-confidence." God really *hears*, but his *answer* to your prayer for restored health means merely this: God gives you greater courage to fight the disease; he does not exert any influence upon the healing processes. He does not interfere with "the laws of nature." Is that a satisfactory conception of prayer? How do you conceive of the relation between prayer and the laws of nature? Another problem: The Bible tells us that all things will happen according to God's plan; then what is the use of praying? Finally, many prayers, seemingly, are never heard; hence, why should we pray?

II. GENERAL OBSERVATIONS ON THE LORD'S PRAYER.

A. CHRIST TAUGHT THIS PRAYER ON MORE THAN ONE OCCASION. Cf. Matt. 6:8-15; Lk. 11:1-4.

B. IN REGARD TO THIS PRAYER WE SHOULD AVOID TWO EXTREMES:

1. To regard it as a ritual, as done in the R. C. Church. Jesus did not tell his disciples to pray nothing but this prayer. It is not to be regarded as a stereotyped method of addressing the Father. Jesus said, *"After this manner . . . . pray ye;"* this prayer is a model.

2. To say that it was "not meant for us," because it does not end with the words, "for Christ's sake." No prayer given by Christ *before his death* could have had such an ending, because the disciples would not have understood these words. On the eve of his passion Jesus teaches his disciples to pray *in his name*, John 16:24; 14:13.

C. IN THIS PRAYER THE ESSENCE OF THE RIGHTEOUSNESS OF THE KINGDOM: THE SECRET DEVOTION OF THE HEART TO GOD IS CLEARLY EXPRESSED; cf. the words of address.

D. Division:

(1) The *Invocation or Address*, "Our Father who art in heaven."

(2) The *Six Petitions:* the first three have a *Godward*, the last three a *manward* reference.

(3) *The Doxology or Conclusion:* "For thine is the kingdom . . . . ."

III. THE INVOCATION: "Our Father who art in heaven."

A. Although even in the O. T. God is spoken of as the Father of his people, yet this concept was not *emphasized* neither *given its full meaning* till this time. The striking thing is that Christ here says, as it were, that the *King* of the kingdom of heaven is at the same time the *Father* of the citizens; they are at the same time *children*. The kingdom is a family.

Questions for Discussion. Does the word "Father," when applied to God in Scripture, always have the same meaning? Just what does it mean here?

B. Notice the use of the plural "Our" instead of "my." This is true throughout the prayer: "Our Father . . . give *us;* forgive *us,*" etc. Lesson: Prayer should never be *selfish;* it should never be on the order of the prayer: "Bless *me* and *my wife; my son* John and his wife; *us four and no more.*" Lesson: the *intercessory* element (voorbede) should not be lacking in our prayers. In this respect also the Lord's prayer is a *model.*

C. In this invocation both God's immanence (his *nearness, his indwelling*) and his transcendence (his *exaltation above the creature*) are expressed. "Our Father" indicates his nearness; he is near to all his children; *infinitely* near; hence with confidence they should come to him with all their needs, wants, and even wishes, providing that these are in harmony with God's revealed will. They need not be *afraid*. God is their Father and *loves* them. Yet, he is the Father *in heaven* (the original reads: "who in the heavens," cf. the Hebrew): hence, the spirit and attitude of reverence should characterize our prayers: he is exalted high above the creature.

QUESTIONS FOR DISCUSSION. Certain evangelists use the pronoun "you" in addressing God. Is that proper? Cf. what you find on p. 287 of *The Tryst* by G. L. Hill.

Moreover, whereas the words, "Our Father," indicate God's *willingness,* nay rather *eagerness* to hear us, the words, "who art in heaven" show his *power* and his *right* (sovereignty) to grant our requests. Finally, reflect again on these words, "Our Father . . . in heaven." They make us feel that we are pilgrims here below; that our *home* is above, in *heaven.* Let us have courage. The child not only wants to be where his Father is; the Father also wants to have his children with him. Then, in heaven we shall forevermore address God as our *Father;* but nevermore shall we have to add, "who art in heaven," *for we shall be with him.*

READING AND STUDY HELPS

We shall first mention several books which offer easy reading material to the average church-member. Be sure, however, to read them *with discretion.*

A. Kuyper, Sr., *To Be Near Unto God;* B. H. Spalink, *The Incense of Prayer;* R. E. Golladay, *Sermons on the Catechism,* vol. III; T. à Kempis, *The Imitation of Christ;* Heidelberg Catechism, Lord's Days 45-52; Kuyper, *E Voto;* J. Bavinck, Ursinus, Thelemann, etc., on the Heid. Catechism; G. A. Kennedy, *The Wicket Gate;* J. O. Buswell, *Problems in Prayer Life;* R. A. Torrey, *How to Pray;* H. W. Adams, etc., *I Cried, He Answered;* D. L. Moody, *Prevailing Prayer;* H. E. Monser, editor of *Cross Reference Bible,* p. 1765, the Biblical data on *Prayer;* any good S. S. Bible, see Index on prayer. L. Trap, art. "Prayer" in *Banner* of Dec. 9, 1932.

Those who wish to make a deeper study we refer to F. W. Grosheide, art "Gebed des Heeren," in *Chr. Enc.;* F. C. Meyster, art. "Bidden" in *Chr. Enc.;* art. "Lord's Prayer" in *I. S. B. E.;* J. G. Gilkey, *Meeting the Challenge of Modern Doubt;* A. B. Bruce, *The Training of the Twelve;* N. Hall, *The Lord's Prayer;* see bibliography at the end of art. "Lord's Prayer" in *I. S. B. E.*

CHAPTER XVI

THE RIGHTEOUSNESS OF THE KINGDOM
Its Essence With Respect to Our Relation to God:

The Secret Devotion of the Heart, Illustrated with Respect to the Lord's Prayer

MATTHEW 6:9b-15.

". . . . Hallowed be thy name. Thy kingdom come. Thy will be done, as in heaven, so on earth. Give us this day our daily bread. And forgive us our debts, as we also have forgiven our debtors. And bring us not into temptation, but deliver us from the evil one. For if ye forgive men their trespasses, your heavenly Father will also forgive you. But if ye forgive not men their trespasses, neither will your Father forgive your trespasses."

NOTE: The King James Version has also the doxology, "For thine is the kingdom, and the power, and the glory, forever. Amen."

We are not going to discuss the authenticity of this doxology. We do not deem that necessary in an outline intended for our Societies.

I. THE FIRST PETITION, "Hallowed be thy name."

A. MEANING: the *name* of God is the revelation of his being. It is probable that Christ has in mind especially the name *Father*. Notice the connection: "Our Father . . . hallowed be thy name." To "*hallow*" God's name means to think, speak, and act in such a manner that *by* us and *through* us our God (as he has revealed himself to us in his names) will be glorified, cf. Ezek. 36:23.

QUESTIONS FOR DISCUSSION. Do we hallow God's name when we worry? Think of what is implied in the name "Father."

We hallow God's name when it hurts us that others (and we ourselves also in a measure) fail to hold God in honor. In view of God's predestinating love; his love revealed, moreover, in the cross; his love to us revealed in establishing with us the covenant of grace; his loving care over us from day to day; his love manifested in even now preparing for us a home in heaven— in view of all that and much more, we love God with a love so intense and deep that we cannot endure to see God's glory disregarded and opposed on every hand. Hence, the prayer, "Hallowed be thy Name." It is a prayer that arises "out of the depths of religious experience." Notice, especially, that the Lord's Prayer does not begin with a petition for our own daily bread, but it *begins and ends with the very specific interests of God's kingdom.* Ps. 148 (the entire Psalm) gives a good commentary on what is meant by "hallowing God's name."

B. GOD'S NAME HALLOWED *BY* US. Meaning, "Father, grant that *we* may hallow thy Name." This implies that we should learn to *know* God's name (i. e., God as he has revealed himself in creation, providence, redemption); especially that we should know him with the knowledge of *experience.*

C. GOD'S NAME HALLOWED THROUGH US. Meaning: "Father, grant that our words and actions may be such that *others* may take us as an example, and honor and glorify thy Name."

QUESTIONS FOR DISCUSSION. What should be our chief aim in life: to glorify God or to "save souls"? Is it possible, however, to separate these two?

II. THE SECOND PETITION. "Thy Kingdom come."

We need not say much about this petition here whereas in a former Chapter we have dwelt in detail on the concept "kingdom." We refer you to that Chapter. Meaning: "Grant that thy kingship may be established in our hearts more and more; that it may also be recognized in every sphere of life: education, government, industry, etc.; and finally, that thy kingdom may soon come with power and glory."

QUESTIONS FOR DISCUSSION. Can we consistently offer this prayer for the coming of God's kingdom, when we are lukewarm in regard to the application of the principles of God's Word to social problems? When we lack enthusiasm for Christian Missions? When we manifest an attitude of apathy or indifference in regard to Christian education? When we love only the members of our own local congregation and not all those who are in Christ? Differentiate between God's essential and Christ's mediatorial kingdom. What connection is there between the first petition and the second; the second and the third?

The deepest wish of the unregenerated heart is: "MY kingdom come." The deepest wish and prayer of the regenerated soul is, "THY kingdom come."

III. THE THIRD PETITION. "Thy will be done, as in heaven, so on earth."

In view of the previous context we hold that

God's *revealed* will, his *law*, is meant here. The meaning of this petition is *not* in the first place: "Grant that we may yield and with joy surrender ourselves to thy *secret* will, thy *plan*, for our lives"; cf. Matt. 26:42; I Pet. 4:19; Acts 21:14; but "Grant that we may obey thy revealed will, and . . . perform the duties of our calling, as willingly and faithfully as the angels in heaven." This implies:

(1) That we must *know* what is God's will for our life. Problem: But God's Word lays down general principles only. How can I know at any definite moment whether I am in the path of obedience to God's will; whether, e. g., I should accept the position offered to me or not?

QUESTIONS FOR DISCUSSION. What do you think of this answer: when *you have prayed that the Lord might reveal his will to you;* and your *conscience* does not offer any objections to the course which you desire to take; and *God's Word* offers no objections; and the *way is opened to you by God's Providence*, then you may conclude that it is God's will that you carry out your plan?

(2) That we should be willing and desirous to *do* God's will. To *know* God's will is not sufficient. By nature we do not want to *do* God's will. By nature our wills are not in conformity with God's will. Hence, an unregenerate man will never *of himself* accept the Gospel. Evangelists often fail to do justice to this fact. Read Phil. 2:13. We should differentiate carefully between:

(*a*) Man's will as it was before the Fall. In conformity with God's will, but able to fall.

(*b*) Man's will after the Fall. At enmity with the will of God.

(*c*) The will of the regenerated man. Two wills warring against one another. See Rom. 7.

(*d*) The will of the redeemed in heaven. Forever in harmony with God's will.

(3) That we should *actually* do God's will. In principle, even here on earth, because of the new life planted in our hearts by the Holy Spirit. But we are never satisfied, for we do not yet obey God's will *as in heaven, i. e., as do the angels and redeemed in heaven.* They obey God's will *always, cheerfully, unhesitatingly, perfectly,* Ps. 103:20, 21.

(4) That we should *promote the doing of God's will by others and in every sphere of life.*

IV. THE FOURTH PETITION. "Give us this day our daily bread."

With this petition we enter the realm of our own physical needs: bread, i.e.,"all things necessary for the body." Read the beautiful explanation given in Lord's Day 50. In this prayer the citizen of the kingdom expresses his absolute dependence upon God, his King and Father. The exact meaning of the words is not very clear. The Dutch has, "Geef ons heden ons *dagelijksch* brood." English: "our *daily* bread." German: "Unser täglich Brod." However, this translation is not the best possible. It changes a petition which has reference to the needs of one day into a prayer which pertains to all time.[1] "Daily bread" means bread for *every day*. But *that* is certainly not what Jesus meant. Others have translated, "Give us this day our *needful* bread." Moffat has, "Give us today our bread for the morrow." The Catholic Douai version has, "our supersubstantial bread," meaning "the Bread of Life," the "supernatural" bread. Although there is as yet no certainty, the best translation of the petition is probably the one given by Grosheide and by Goodspeed, *"Give us today bread for the day."* Christ teaches his hearers to pray that they may have bread for the day which has begun. Needless to say that this prayer for *bread* is, by implication, a prayer for *work*, in order that we may *earn* our bread. This little petition combines two ideas very beautifully:

(*a*) The bread is entirely a *gift* which we receive of God's *grace*. Hence, *"Give* us."

(*b*) At the same time the bread is in a sense *our* bread, i. e., we *work* for it, and we *accept it with gratitude*.

QUESTION FOR DISCUSSION. Jesus here teaches us to pray for bread; hence, for *work*. Should we, as Christians, pray for a return of the prosperity of former days? In which way should we "fight the depression"?

This prayer for "bread" is a prayer for "bread with God's blessing upon it." It teaches us to *trust* in God; hence we are taught to pray for "bread for this day" only.

V. THE FIFTH PETITION. "And forgive us our debts, as we also have forgiven our debtors."

"For if ye forgive men their trespasses, your

heavenly Father will also forgive you. But if ye forgive not men their trespasses, neither will your Father forgive your trespasses."

A. Debts and Trespasses. In the N. T. we find at least ten different words for sin. One means "missing the mark"; another "disobedience"; further: "lawlessness," "transgression," "error," "fault," etc. Of the two words used here in our passage one is "debt," i. e., failure to meet our obligation with respect to God; the other is "trespass," i. e., deviation. The original word signifies a "falling beside," when "a man having reached an acknowledged pitch of godliness falls back from it;"[2] we might say "temporary backsliding."

B. "Forgive us . . . as we . . ." Jesus does *not* mean that when we forgive men their trespasses, we thereby *earn* God's forgiveness; neither does he mean that God will forgive us only *in the measure in which* we forgive others; but he means that we should forgive men their trespasses *after the manner in which* God forgives us our trespasses, i. e., by returning good for evil, love for hatred.[3]

C. An unforgiving heart does not receive pardon for the simple reason that it *cannot*.

VI. THE SIXTH PETITION. "And bring us not into temptation, but deliver us from the evil one."

Meaning, not merely: cause us to remain standing while we are in temptation; but grant that we may not even enter into the temptation of Satan, i. e., cause us not to fall into Satan's hands; rather, deliver us from that evil one; cf. II Sam. 24:14.

VII. THE DOXOLOGY. "For thine is the kingdom, and the power, and the glory forever. Amen."

"Thine is the kingdom," i. e., thou hast the *authority, the right* to grant our petitions. "Thine is the power," i. e., thou hast the *strength, the might, the ability* to fulfil our needs. "Thine is the glory," a glory which is especially "the glory of his *grace*," Eph. 1:6, i. e., thou art *gracious; hence, willing, yea, desirous* to hear us. The word "Amen" expresses the conviction on the part of the believer that his prayer will be heard.

REFERENCES
1) GROSHEIDE, op. cit., p. 74.
2) R. C. TRENCH, *Synonyms of the N. T.*, p. 231.
3) GROSHEIDE, op. cit., p. 76.

READING AND STUDY HELPS
Same as for previous chapter, which see.

CHAPTER XVII

THE RIGHTEOUSNESS OF THE KINGDOM
Its Essence With Respect to Our Relation to God:

The Secret Devotion of the Heart, Illustrated with Respect to Fasting

MATTHEW 6:16-18.
> "Moreover, when ye fast, be not, as the hypocrites, of a sad countenance: for they disfigure their faces, that they may be seen of men to fast. Verily I say unto you, They have received their reward. But thou, when thou fastest, anoint thy head, and wash thy face; that thou be not seen of men to fast, but of thy Father who is in secret: and thy Father, who seeth in secret, shall recompense thee."

I. GENERAL REMARKS ABOUT FASTING.

A. Definition: Fasting means partial or total abstinence from food for a certain period of time for the purpose of the mortification of the body (i. e., the appetites) and the humiliation of the soul. It is a religious discipline.

B. Fasting, as a religious rite, is found almost everywhere. In some religions fasting is made binding, and public fasts are definitely appointed. In others it is voluntary. The Mohammedans observe a fast "while it is light during the month Ramadhan."[1] The five pillars of Islam are faith, prayer, fasting, almsgiving, and the pilgrimage.

C. Connection between fasting and spiritual life. This relation may be briefly expressed as follows: "The continually stuffed body cannot see spiritual things." When we are continually thinking about food and drink, about material things, we are prone to forget about the interests of the soul. Hence, the value of fasting.

D. Purposes of fasting. People fast in order:

(*a*) thereby to express their grief in bereavement, I Sam. 31:13; II Sam. 1:12;

(*b*) their sorrow in times of great distress and calamity, I Sam. 1:7;

(*c*) repentance from sin, either personal or national, I Kings 21:27; Neh. 9:1;

(*d*) to prepare themselves for great tasks, Ezra 8:21 ff;

(*e*) to enjoy the uninterrupted communion with God, Ex. 34:28; Matt. 4:2;

(*f*) to concentrate their attention on the condition of the soul; for the purpose, therefore, of *humiliation.*

E. The Jews kept (and even today the orthodox Jews keep) many fasts: fasts in commemoration of the siege of Jerusalem; of the murder of Gedaliah; of the destruction of the Temple; of the capture of Jerusalem, etc. These fasts were not prescribed in the Law.

F. *Yet, there was one prescribed annual Fast,* namely, *the Great Day of Atonement.* Ex. 30:10; Lev. 16:1-34; 23:26-32; Num. 29:7-11. "And it shall be a statute forever unto you: in the seventh month, on the tenth day of the month, ye shall afflict your souls, and shall do no manner of work . . . for on this day shall atonement be made for you, to cleanse you; *from all your sins shall ye be clean before Jehovah* . . . ."

G. It is very plain that this one great Fast pointed forward to the redemption which is in Christ. Read Lev. 16. Notice that one goat symbolically *bears away* the sins of the people; the other one *is sacrificed* for their sins. Together they point to Christ who himself bore our sin in his body on the tree, who "took away the sin of the world," and who "died for our sins." Hence, *it is plain that we are not REQUIRED to fast now. The one fast which was prescribed in the O. T. was fulfilled on the cross.* Cf. also Matt. 9:14-17. Consider this passage carefully.

H. Jesus, in the passage we are studying, does not condemn fasting as such, but only the superfluous, ostentatious, and supposedly meritorious fasts of the scribes and Pharisees, "to be seen of men."

I. Fasting as such is nowhere condemned. Jesus himself fasted, Matt. 4:2; Mark 9:29; so did Paul, Acts 9:9; II Cor. 6:5; cf. Acts 13:2, 3; 14:23. Over against the supposedly meritorious fasts of Roman Catholics, the Reformers advocated Scriptural fasts "to bridle or subdue the flesh and to discipline the spirit." Our forefathers fasted in connection with wars and public calamities. Dr. A. Kuyper, Sr., and Dr. H. Bavinck have also defended the voluntary fast for purposes of meditation and humiliation. Conclusion: for us there are no prescribed days of fasting; nevertheless, it is perfectly permissible for us to fast, i. e., to the honor of God.

II. THE FAST OF THE HYPOCRITES. "Moreover, when ye fast, be not, as the hypocrites, of a sad countenance: for they disfigure their faces, that they may be seen of men to fast. Verily I say unto you, They have received their reward."

Meaning: The scribes and Pharisees not only held the customary public fasts but, in order to show everybody how pious they were, they also kept private fasts. They fasted regularly on Thursdays and Mondays, the days on which Moses was believed to have gone up to, and returned from, Mount Sinai. Moreover, on these days they would purposely disfigure their faces so that every one might see that they were fasting, and might honor them for this. Some modern beggars will disfigure themselves in order to excite sympathy, especially in Oriental lands. For the statement, "They have received their reward," see a previous Chapter.

III. THE FAST OF THE CITIZENS OF THE KINGDOM. "But thou, when thou fastest, anoint thy head, and wash thy face; that thou be not seen of men to fast, but of thy Father who is in secret: and thy Father, who seeth in secret, shall recompense thee."

1. "But thou when thou fastest." This plainly implies that, although fasting is not *pre-*

scribed for us, neither is it *forbidden*. It is at times very helpful.

2. "Anoint thy head, and wash thy face." In other words: conceal your fasts. Your fasting must be kept sacred and secret. Here again Jesus emphasizes the *essence of the righteousness of the kingdom of God, namely, the secret devotion of the heart.*

3. "And thy Father," etc. We have explained this clause previously.

IV. CHRIST'S TEACHING ON FASTING APPLIED TO OUR DAY:

A. The chief purpose of "fasting" was humiliation. That is required even today.

QUESTION FOR DISCUSSION. What is your attitude toward days of humiliation and prayer in view of great calamities?

B. Fasting also implied "self-denial." Are we practicing this today?

QUESTIONS FOR DISCUSSION. Is it proper for a Christian to spend money for cigars for his own enjoyment while he neglects to support the church, Christian education, and missions? Could we not practice more self-denial? The Jews, in fasting, denied themselves food; should we not deny ourselves luxuries?

C. Fasting, moreover, served the purpose of affording greater opportunity for meditation. That also holds for us. Do we practice it sufficiently?

D. Fasting, as interpreted by Christ, emphasized the necessity of the *secret devotion of the heart to God.*

E. Fasting, as interpreted by Christ, points to the fact that the Christian's outlook on life should be optimistic. He should "anoint his head and wash his face."

REFERENCES
1) J. A. MAYNARD, *The Living Religions of the World*, pp. 123, 125.

READING AND STUDY HELPS
Commentaries on the S. on the Mt., and on Matthew, previously mentioned. Art. "Fasting" in *Encyclopedia Brit.;* Ds. J. Jansen, art. "Vasten" in *Chr. Enc.;* L. Berkhof, *Biblical Archæology,* pp. 90, 169 ff.; Articles "Fast," "Fasting," "Fasts and Feasts," in *I. S. B. E.*

CHAPTER XVIII

THE RIGHTEOUSNESS OF THE KINGDOM
Its Essence With Respect to Our Relation to God:

Undivided Trust in God
Trust in God versus Mammon Worship

MATTHEW 6:19-24.
"Lay not up for yourselves treasures upon the earth, where moth and rust consume, and where thieves break through and steal: but lay up for yourselves treasures in heaven, where neither moth nor rust doth consume, and where thieves do not break through nor steal: for where thy treasure is, there will thy heart be also. The lamp of the body is the eye: if, therefore, thine eye be single, thy whole body shall be full of light. But if thine eye be evil, thy whole body shall be full of darkness. If, therefore, the light that is in thee be darkness, how great is the darkness! ..No man can serve two masters: for either he will hate the one, and love the other; or else he will hold to one, and despise the other. Ye cannot serve God and mammon."

I. CONNECTION.

By way of review it is necessary to remind ourselves of the fact that in the section of the S. on the Mt. which we are now studying, Christ is discussing the *essence of the righteousness of the kingdom*. It may be expressed in these words: "Love God above all and your neighbor as yourself." We are now studying the meaning of "loving God above all." Christ views this love from two angles:

The Sermon on the Mount 157

(1) as the *secret devotion of the heart* (over against the ostentatious and vainglorious display of outward works by the scribes and Pharisees). That secret devotion of the heart to our heavenly Father should be evident, e. g., in almsgiving, in prayer, and in fasting. But in the passage which we are to study in *this* and the next two Chapters, Christ views that love with reference to God from another angle; he views it now:

(2) as *undivided trust in God:* trust in God versus Mammon worship; trust in God versus worry; trust in God based on God's promises. The first of these three (i. e., trust in God versus Mammon worship) we shall now discuss:

II. THE PROHIBITION. "Lay not up for yourselves treasures upon the earth."

A. Meaning:

1. Literally Jesus said, "Do not continue to treasure treasures for yourselves upon the earth." In other words, Jesus knew that his hearers were already guilty of this very evil.[1] They had been storing up earthly treasures. Christ tells them to break with this bad habit.

2. Jesus does not refer *exclusively* to gold or silver. Your "treasure" may be an object which to other people is entirely worthless. In the mind of Jesus a treasure is "that which draws the heart after it," whatever that may be.

3. Yet, the words, "upon the earth," and the references to "moth," "rust," and "thieves," plainly indicate that Jesus is thinking *especially*

(though not *exclusively*, see 2) of such treasures as superfluous apparel, precious metals, vessels filled with coins buried in the earth (there were no banks), etc.

QUESTIONS FOR DISCUSSION. Does Jesus forbid all saving of money? In the words, "Lay not up *for yourself* treasures upon the earth," do you see an argument for communism? In days of hardship even some Christians advocate communism as found e. g., in Russia. What is the fundamental difference between communism as found there and communism as found, e. g., in Acts 2:44, and as advocated in the Sermon on the Mount? In the light of the words of Jesus which we are studying, what is your attitude toward capitalism? Just what can we do, as Christians, besides "praying for better times"? Is money *"the* root of all evil?" Cf. I Tim. 6:10 (original); Eph. 5:5; Col. 3:5.

B. GROUNDS OR REASONS WHY WE SHOULD NOT LAY UP TREASURES UPON THE EARTH:

1. Because Christ said so. He is our Lord and Sovereign.

2. Because those treasures will perish. "Moth and rust will consume them. Thieves will break through and steal them." The moth eats into the silken treasures of the East; and through the wall of clay (of an Oriental house) the thief easily digs an entrance and he steals the ill-guarded vessel filled with gold.

3. Because you yourself will soon die, leaving your treasure behind. The words of Jesus remind us of that passage in Job. 13:28, "Though I am like a rotten thing that consumeth, like a garment *that is moth-eaten."* Says Dykes, "When death takes a man's breath away, it takes his purse as well; disinherits him of his

lands; unrobes him of earthly raiment; and despatches him, lonely, naked, shivery, a poor despoiled ghost, into the unknown."[2]

4. Because the very heaping up of worldly wealth causes men to love it, and draws them away from God. Again quoting Dykes, "The fortune which a busy man toils late and early to augment, and for the sake of which his head has been blanched with anxiety; or the estate which is purchased at the expense of what ought to have been patrimony to his younger children . . . . these possessions have acquired a fictitions dearness through the heavy price which they have cost."[3] That is the meaning of, "For where thy treasure is, there will thy heart be also."

5. Because these treasures darken the soul, and draw it away from God. "The lamp of the body is the eye." Jesus does not mean that the eye is the source of light for our body, but that it is, as it were, the light-bringer, the guide. If it were not for your eye, you would not be able to make proper use of your hands and feet. You might stumble, like the blind. Hence, if your eye be "single," i. e., good, so that both eyes concentrate on one object; if you can "see straight," your whole body shall be full of light: well-governed. But if your eye is "bad," i. e., diseased, your whole body will be full of darkness: not able to function properly. Now even as we have a physical eye, so we have a spiritual eye, an eye that looks upward, and sees God. But if that "eye" or that "light" which is "in you,"

i. e., in your soul, be darkened, i. e., if it be darkened by your passion for earthly treasures, then how great must be the darkness of your soul (its very "eye" having been darkened)!

6. Because these treasures enslave the will. "No man can serve two masters . . . ." Says Dykes, "The service of which Jesus spoke . . . *was the utter subjection of a bond-slave to the mere will*—the almost unchecked caprice—*of a slave-lord.*"4) Hence, it was entirely impossible for a slave to serve two masters. So, if we serve Mammon, i. e., wealth, then Mammon will become our sole Master. We cannot serve God also. We must choose.

III. THE COMMAND. "But lay up for yourselves treasures in heaven, where neither moth nor rust doth consume, and where thieves do not break through nor steal."

Study, in this connection, Lk. 16:9. (Meaning: Use your money for missions and charitable purposes; the money so used will bring you "friends" in the Lord; then by and when "it," i. e., your earthly wealth, shall fail you, and you shall exchange this life for the better life, these very friends will receive you into the eternal tabernacles: will welcome you into heaven). *By simple trust in God and liberal giving to his causes we lay up for ourselves treasures in heaven, for God will reward us.* I Pet. 4:5 offers an excellent commentary on this command of Christ. The treasure in heaven is never stolen; does not waste away; its beauty does not even fade. Nay, on the contrary, in a sense we can say that it is an ever-increasing inheritance.

REFERENCES
1) A. T. ROBERTSON, *A Grammar of the Greek N. T. in the Light of Historical Research*, fourth ed., p. 853.
2) J. O. DYKES, *The Relations of the Kingdom*, p. 24.
3) *Same*, p. 30.
4) *Same*, p. 39.

READING AND STUDY HELPS
First of all and most of all I wish to refer to the beautiful exposition of this entire passage given by J. O. Dykes in his *Relations of the Kingdom*. I have not been able to find anything that equals it. Further: see the various commentaries mentioned in Outline I.

CHAPTER XIX

THE RIGHTEOUSNESS OF THE KINGDOM
Its Essence With Respect to Our Relation to God

Undivided Trust in God
Trust in God versus Worry

MATTHEW 6:25-32.
"Therefore I say unto you, Be not anxious for your life, what ye shall eat, or what ye shall drink; nor yet for your body, what ye shall put on. Is not the life more than the food, and the body than raiment? Behold the birds of the heaven, that they sow not neither do they reap, nor gather into barns; and your heavenly Father feedeth them. Are not ye of much more value than they? And which of you by being anxious can add one cubit unto the measure of his life? And why are ye anxious concerning raiment? Consider the lilies of the field, how they grow; they toil not, neither do they spin: yet I say unto you, that even Solomon in all his glory was not arrayed like one of these. But if God doth so clothe the grass of the field, which today is, and tomorrow is cast into the oven, shall he not much more clothe you, O ye of little faith? Be not therefore anxious, saying, What shall we eat? or, What shall we drink? or, Wherewithal shall we be clothed? For after all these things do the Gentiles seek; for your heavenly Father knoweth that ye have need of all these things."

LUKE 12:22-30.
"And he said unto his disciples, Therefore I say unto you, Be not anxious for your life, what ye shall eat; nor yet for your body, what ye shall put on. For the life is more than the food, and the body than the raiment. Consider THE RAVENS, that they sow not, neither reap; which have no store-chamber nor barn; and God feed-

eth them: of how much more value are ye than the birds! And which of you by being anxious can add a cubit unto the measure of his life? IF THEN YE ARE NOT ABLE TO DO THAT WHICH IS LEAST, why are ye anxious concerning the rest? Consider the lilies, how they grow: they toil not, neither do they spin; yet I say unto you, Even Solomon in all his glory was not arrayed like one of these. But if God doth so clothe the grass in the field, which to-day is, and to-morrow is cast into the oven: how much more shall he clothe you, O ye of little faith? And seek not ye what ye shall eat, and what ye shall drink, NEITHER BE YE OF DOUBTFUL MIND. For all these things do the nations of the world seek after: but your Father knoweth that ye have need of these things."

I. CONNECTION.

The passage of the Sermon on the Mount which we study in this Chapter is by common consent one of the most touchingly beautiful sayings of Jesus. It has been quoted, read, interpreted, and misinterpreted more often, perhaps, than any other part of the Sermon with the exception of The Lord's Prayer and the Beatitudes. In order to grasp to some extent the exquisite beauty of the thought expressed here, it is necessary that we dwell for a moment on the connection in which it occurs.

Christ is discussing the righteousness of the Kingdom of heaven. He has pointed out that it does not consist in a vain-glorious display of works, but in *trust, i. e., complete confidence in* and *self-surrender to* the heavenly Father. This attitude of trust is incompatible with the arduous attempt to acquire treasures on earth. In the measure in which a man has his eyes riveted on earthly wealth he will be blind to the spiritual treasures. Hence, inasmuch as earthly treasures darken the soul and enslave the will, one should not "continue to treasure up treasures for himself upon the earth."

Does this mean that only those who have actually amassed a vast store of earthly goods, or are busy doing so, are guilty? Lest any one should think this, Jesus now proceeds to tell his hearers in words of tender admonition (because they concern the poor rather than the rich?) that the attitude of *anxiety because of earthly goods which seem to be out of reach* (food and clothing which one fears are not forthcoming) and the attitude of *avarice manifested by the person who has acquired or is busily engaged in the acquisition of earthly possessions,* spring from the same root: *lack of trust* (at least: incomplete trust) *in God, the Father; appraising earthly goods above heavenly: material above spiritual.* Both avarice and anxiety *lead away from* (instead of *to*) God. Both darken the eye of the soul, so that it cannot see spiritual verities. Both enslave the will. "Therefore," . . . be not anxious for your life.

II. THE MEANING OF CHRIST'S EXHORTATION. "Therefore I say unto you, Be not anxious for your life, what ye shall eat, or what ye shall drink; nor yet for your body, what ye shall put on."

A. "BE NOT ANXIOUS . . . ." The readers are perhaps better acquainted with the A. V. than with the Revised. Now the A. V. offers a "most unhappy mistranslation" of this passage. It tells us that we should not "take thought" for our life. Now that is not at all what Jesus said. "To take thought" (zorgen) is one thing; "to be filled with anxiety," i. e., to fret and worry, and become restless and feverish (bezorgd zijn) is quite another thing. Scripture very clearly commands us to do the one, Prov. 6:6; 30:25; II Cor. 12:14; I Tim. 5:8 ("But if any provideth not for his own, and specially his own household, he hath denied the faith, and is worse than an unbeliever"). It also very clearly teaches us not to do the other. Literally Jesus says, "Stop being anxious about your life," etc.

B. ". . . . FOR YOUR LIFE, WHAT YE SHALL EAT, OR WHAT YE SHALL DRINK, NOR YET FOR YOUR BODY, WHAT YE SHALL PUT ON."

Jesus *mentions* only food, drink, and clothing. Does he mean that one may worry about all the other things, e. g., a student about an examination, a sick person about an operation, a candidate for a political office about the position he cherishes, a candidate for the ministry about a "call," etc.? If we should so interpret the words of Jesus, we would misinterpret them. Jesus militated against this crassly literal method of interpreting his words throughout his sojourn on earth, John 2:19; 3:3-5; 4:10; 4:32; 6:52, 53; 11:11, 12; 14:4; Matt. 16:6, etc. Then, what *does* he mean? This: that we should not be filled with over-anxiety with respect to whatever we may deem *indispensable* or at least *very desirable*. Food and raiment offer the best symbol of all these things which we deem necessary for our future happiness. Hence, in these words of Jesus *all worry or anxiety with a view to the future is condemned.*

III. THE GROUNDS UPON WHICH IT RESTS.

A. *Anxiety leads away from God, blinds the spiritual eye, enslaves the will to Mammon.* See under I; also Chapter XVIII. This ground is implied in the word "Therefore."

B. *It is FOOLISH.* (For ease of memorization we have grouped the following three reasons why one should not worry under three words beginning with F: foolish, fruitless, faithless). It is foolish because God, the Father, will certainly provide for his children:

1. *This follows logically from the fact that God is our Creator.* "Is not the life more than the food, and the body than raiment?" Meaning: the God who created our living bodies will certainly sustain his own handiwork. He who created *life* (the greater) will certainly provide the *means* (the less: food and clothing) which are necessary to sustain life. Creation and providence constitute *one* divine work.

QUESTIONS FOR DISCUSSION. Did God rest or did He work on the seventh day? Criticize the question. Just what is the difference between God's *creative* activity, on the one hand, and his work of *preservation, co-operation, and government,* on the other? God, the Creator, will certainly provide for His children. How then do you explain the presence of death on such an enormous scale in the universe at large and even among God's children. Remember that in the sphere of sentient creatures God's providence is not realized *mechanically*. Reflect on the *purpose* of death for the believer.

2. *It also follows from the fact that God cares for that part of creation which lies below the human level (birds and lilies). Hence, he will certainly care for his children.* "Behold the birds of the heaven that they sow not, neither do they reap . . . and your heavenly Father feedeth them. Are not ye of much more value than they . . And why are ye anxious concerning raiment? Consider the lilies of the field how they grow; they toil not, neither do they spin; yet . . . even Solomon in all his glory was not arrayed like one of these . . . ." Notice:

    a. "THE BIRDS OF THE HEAVEN." Jesus referred to the same species of birds which even today exist in Palestine. Because of their joyful songs, gay colors, and powerful flight birds are often referred to in Scripture. Cf. Gen. 7:14, 15; 15:9-11; Lev. 1:14-17; 12:8; 14:4-8; Num. 6:10; Job 41:5 (cf. 12:7); Ps. 11:1; 50:11; 84:3; 148:10; Eccl. 10:20; Song of Solomon 2:12; Is. 18:6; 46:11; Jer. 4:25; 12:9; 19:7; Ezek. 39:4, 17; Hos. 9:11; Matt. 13:4; Mk. 4:32; Rev. 19:17, 21, etc. The Gospel of Luke mentions the ravens. Christ may have pointed to the ravens, pigeons, field-sparrows, swallows, and/or meadow-larks, flying past on careless wing, confident that their search for food would be rewarded.

    b. "THE LILIES OF THE FIELD." Goodspeed translates "wild flowers." The word used in the original may refer to almost any kind of wild flower. It may refer to hyacinths, tulips, irises, gladioli, narcissi, etc. Yet, although the word as such has this general connotation, the fact that Christ calls particular attention to the "beauty" and the "rapid growth" of certain field-flowers renders it probable that he was pointing to the great huleh lilies of Palestine, "the most gorgeous and beautiful of all the flowers growing there."[1]

c. "BEHOLD THE BIRDS ..... CONSIDER (i. e., study *closely*) THE LILIES."

QUESTIONS FOR DISCUSSION. At times we meet with Christians who seem to have an aversion to the study of science. Is that the proper attitude? Think of the words of Jesus. Christ certainly took delight in the study of nature. Cf. Matt. 16:2; Lk. 12:54; Matt. 24:32; John 15:1-6; Matt. 23:37; 26:34, etc.

d. "THEY (the birds) SOW NOT, NEITHER DO THEY REAP ... THEY (the lilies) TOIL NOT NEITHER DO THEY SPIN." Christ's argument is this: "If the birds and the lilies which cannot toil and work for self-preservation and which cannot take thought have no reason for worry; then certainly we, who can both work and take thought for the future, have no reason to be filled with anxiety. Again, if God even provides for these "lower" creatures, how much more will he care for those who not only have been created in his own image, but who by grace trust in him!"

QUESTION FOR DISCUSSION. Do the words of Jesus imply a condemnation of life insurance?

e. "YOUR HEAVENLY FATHER FEEDETH THEM." Notice: *your* ... Father. Christ clearly distinguishes between God's relation to all his creatures and his relation to his own spiritual children. *Their Creator* is *your Father*. If *their Creator* thus provides for them, then certainly *your Father* will provide for you. To worry is foolish, therefore.

f. "... EVEN SOLOMON IN ALL HIS GLORY WAS NOT ARRAYED LIKE ONE OF THESE." Jesus does not indulge in hyperbole (figurative exaggeration) when he says this. The finest garment Solomon ever possessed was sackcloth compared to the beauty of the lily. "For the dress of man .... can be nothing more than *borrowed* as to its material, and *imitated* as to its coloring; *borrowed* from the plant's stem or from the worm's cocoon; *imitated* from the radiant colors which ... glow among the grass in the wild flower's crown of splendour."[2]

g. ".... IF GOD SO CLOTHE THE GRASS WHICH TODAY IS, AND TOMORROW IS CAST INTO THE OVEN ....." Says Mackie, "The time when Palestine looks greenest and most beautiful is the beginning of April [i. e., about the time when this sermon was preached, see Chapter I]. There is then a great simultaneous outburst of flowers .... This *sudden* greenness of landscape.... rapidly disappears.... This fact of climate enters into frequent allusion to the brevity of life ...."[3] These flowering "grasses" (i. e., plants) were cut down in order to serve as fuel for the domestic oven in a land where fuel was not plentiful.

h. ".... SHALL HE NOT MUCH MORE CLOTHE YOU, O YE OF LITTLE FAITH?" There is a double argument here. It runs somewhat as follows:

(1) If God even provides for the lowly and short-lived *lilies,* then he will *surely* care for his *own children!*

(2) If God decks the lilies with such very *beautiful garments,* then he *surely* will give unto his children the *ordinary garments* which they need!

C. *It is FRUITLESS.* "AND WHICH OF YOU BY BEING ANXIOUS CAN ADD ONE CUBIT TO THE MEASURE OF HIS LIFE?" Not *"to his stature,"* as the A. V. has. That certainly would not be a little thing. Christ means, "You may be worrying about a tomorrow which you will never see. You cannot add to your days." Cf. Ps. 39:6. A man may "worry himself to *death*"; he cannot worry himself into *a longer span of life.*

D. *It is FAITHLESS.* "BE NOT THEREFORE ANXIOUS SAYING, WHAT SHALL WE EAT OR WHAT SHALL WE DRINK . . . FOR AFTER ALL THESE THINGS DO THE GENTILES SEEK; FOR YOUR HEAVENLY FATHER KNOWETH THAT YE HAVE NEED OF ALL THESE THINGS." Notice:

1. Faith and worry cannot *consistently* dwell together; for the man who worries *doubts* (see Luke) God's ability or willingness to provide.

2. Christians should be *distinctive*. By worrying about material things they lose their distinctiveness, and become like the heathen, for that is exactly what they do.

3. Although Christ admonishes his disciples, and plainly teaches that worry is sin, nevertheless he also clearly indicates that even those "of

little faith" (i. e., those who do worry at times, but who fight against it) are the object of God's tender love.

4. "Your Father . . . knoweth." That is all that is necessary. His "knowledge" implies "care."

REFERENCES
1) G. C. MORGAN, *The Gospel According to Matthew*, page 68.

2) J. O. DYKES, *The Relations of the Kingdom*, pages 69. 70.

3) G. M. MACKIE, *Bible Manners and Customs*, page 22.

READING AND STUDY HELPS
Articles "Lilies," "Flowers," "Birds" in *I. S. B. E.* "Lelie" in *Chr. Encyclopaedie.* See under "Birds and Fowls" in *The Cross Reference Bible* or any good S. S. Bible. Books have been written on the Plants and Birds of Scripture. Further, G. M. Mackie, *Bible Manners and Customs* (an inexpensive and very useful book). A. Maclaren has a very good sermon on Luke 12:23-31 (though we do not agree with all his conclusions). See esp. G. C. Morgan, *The Gospel According to Matthew*, p. 67 ff. Further, books previously referred to. Also, G. Brillenburg Wurth's *De Bergrede en Onze Tijd*, pp. 93-99.

CHAPTER XX

THE RIGHTEOUSNESS OF THE KINGDOM
Its Essence With Respect to Our Relation to God
Undivided Trust in God
Trust in God Based on God's Promise

MATTHEW 6:33, 34.
> "But seek ye first his kingdom, and his righteousness; and all these things shall be added unto you. Be not therefore anxious for the morrow; for the morrow will be anxious for itself. Sufficient unto the day is the evil thereof."

I. INTRODUCTION.

We are living in days of divine visitation. The walls of our economic house are tottering; its foundations crumbling. Divine ordinances which have been honored by many generations are severely criticized by some, openly ridiculed by others. The *"faith* of our fathers" is becoming more and more the "faith of our *fathers."* In view of all these distressing facts is it any wonder that many Christians are filled with anxiety when they think of the future, their own future, and the future (both spiritual and material) of their children? Now, the passage which we studied in the previous Chapter indicated clearly that all such worry is sinful. That it is foolish, fruitless, and faithless. Instead of worrying, the citizens of the Kingdom should *trust*. But, at this point you raise the question, "Why should we trust? Does Scripture warrant such peace of mind? Does it offer any solid ground upon which we may safely rear the structure of our confidence?" The answer is contained in the passage which we are to study in this Chapter. Our reliance upon God is *definitely based on God's covenant-promise: all these things shall be added unto you.* This week's lesson contains: (1) The command or exhortation. Unless this command is obeyed, the promise will not be realized. (2) The promise. (3) The prohibition or dehortation.

II. THE EXHORTATION. *"But seek ye first his Kingdom and his righteousness."*

A. "But seek ye . . . ."

Notice the contrast: verse 32, "For after all these things do the *Gentiles seek* . . ."; verse 33, "But *seek ye* first his kingdom." The Gentiles are absorbed in the things which pertain to this earth. The citizens of the Kingdom should apply all their energies to the great task of taking possession of the Kingdom of heaven. From this it becomes clear that faith is not a purely passive attitude. It is not merely a "being moved." The essence of religion is not fully expressed in the term "the feeling of absolute dependence upon God" (Schleiermacher, though his definitions vary and sometimes indicate an active delight). Pillar-saints, ascetics, mystics, and pietists—there are many even today—have forgotten this. Men "enter violently" into the

Kingdom, Luke 16:16 (R. V.); they "crowd" into it (Goodspeed); they "press" into it (Moffatt); they *strive* to enter in by the *narrow* door, Luke 13:24; cf. Matt. 7:13. True religion, saving faith, implies the highest kind of activity.

The question is asked, "But do we not find another representation in this very Sermon on the Mount? Namely, that the Kingdom of heaven must be received as a *gift* out of the hand of the Father? Matt. 5:3-12." We answer: these two views do not contradict but they complement each other. Let us illustrate:

Of itself the little plant has no nutriment. Its roots and leaves are the empty hands stretched out to the Giver: Environment, i. e., soil, air, sunshine, and rain. How completely dependent is the little plant upon its Environment! In itself it does not even have the power by means of which its roots and leaves absorb nutriment. The energy of the sunlight must furnish the plant with this power. It receives its nourishment as a *gift*, therefore. But does this mean that the plant is *inactive?* Not at all. Those roots and leaves, though completely *receptive and dependent*, are wonderfully *active*. It has been calculated that the amount of work done by a large tree in a single day to raise water and minerals from the soil to the leaves is equal to the amount of energy expended by a person who carries three hundred pailfuls of water, two at a time, up a ten-foot flight of stairs. Those little roots absorb water and minerals from the soil, and through an inner canal conduct these upward to the leaves. Those leaves, through their *stomata,* take carbon dioxide from the air; convert carbon dioxide, water, minerals, to sugar and protein, and through an outer canal send these downward.

The same is true with respect to the believer. He receives the Kingdom of heaven as a *gift,* indeed. He does not, in Ritschlian fashion, *establish* or *create* this kingdom. It is *God's* Kingdom, *given* to the believer. Yet, after the new principle of life has been imparted unto him by means of regeneration, he becomes very active; that new principle of life is an *active* principle; he now begins to "work out his own salvation with fear and trembling" just because "it is God who worketh in him both to will and to work for his good pleasure." Phil. 2:12. He "presses on, if so be that he may lay hold on that for which also he was laid hold on by Christ Jesus," Phil. 3:12. His mind accepts God's truth; his heart drinks in God's love; his will surrenders itself to and becomes actively engaged in doing God's will. Salvation is by *grace* (i. e., a free *gift*) through *faith* (*active* self-surrender).

B. "But seek ye HIS KINGDOM AND HIS RIGHTEOUSNESS."

1. Meaning: Strive with all that is in you to make God King in your heart and life; hence, also in the hearts and lives of others, and in every sphere of life: education, government, industry, science, etc. See Chapter II for the term "kingdom."

2. God's Kingdom (recognized sovereignty in the heart and life of the believer, etc.) and righteousness (loving God above all; hence, the secret devotion of the heart to God and undivided trust in him, with love toward the neighbor) are one and inseparable. The two terms express the same thing from different angles. Hence, at times the Sermon on the Mount represents it thus: that righteousness comes first, Matt. 5:20; at other times, e. g., in the passage which we are studying, we find the opposite order. Solution: "the Kingdom of God *is righteousness*," Rom. 14:17.

3. Notice: "and HIS righteousness." It is *his* righteousness because it is in sharp contrast with the righteousness of scribes and Pharisees, as has been shown abundantly. It is *his* righteousness because it is not man-made or man-discovered but a gift which the sinner receives out of his hand. Those who claim that the Sermon on the Mount differs essentially from the teachings of Paul would do well to compare these words of Jesus with Rom. 3:22; Phil. 3:9. The similarity of expression and thought is very striking.

C. "BUT SEEK YE FIRST . . . ."

According to the context, the meaning is *not:* Seek ye *first* the Kingdom of God and his righteousness, and *afterward* these material things. Just the opposite: you will not need to *seek* (thirst after, be completely absorbed in the search for) these material things; they will be "added unto you."

QUESTIONS FOR DISCUSSION. According to these words of Jesus, what should be *first:* tuition, so that our children may attend the Christian School where there is one, or a new radio or piece of furniture? Are "seeking the kingdom of God and his righteousness" and "providing for the *needs* of the family" two separate pursuits, or does the one imply the other?

III. THE PROMISE. ". . . . AND ALL THESE THINGS SHALL BE ADDED UNTO YOU."

A. This promise is realized only in the lives of those who seek first the Kingdom of God and his righteousness. It is the promise of the *covenant of grace.* By the expression "all these things" is meant all things which we *need* (see explanation of verses 25-32), represented under the symbol of food, drink, and clothing. Our *seeking* and God's *giving* cannot be separated. The emphasis is here upon things which are necessary for the sustenance of our *body.* As this promise is *conditional* (realized only in the lives of those who seek first the Kingdom of God and his righteousness), and made to *believers* (see verse 30: ye of *little* faith; even little faith is faith), it is evident that Christ is speaking about the covenant-promise. The essence of the covenant-promise is, "I will be a God unto thee and unto thy seed after thee." Cf. Gen. 17:7, 8; Ex. 20:2; Deut. 5:2, 3, 6; Jer. 24:7; 30:22; 31:33; Ezek. 11:20; Zech. 13:9; Matt. 13:17; Rom. 4:22; II Cor. 6:16; Rev. 21:3, etc. We find it throughout the Word of God. Let no one say that Christ is here giving a promise which has nothing to do with the covenant inasmuch as the latter refers to *spiritual,* Christ's promise to *ma-*

terial blessings. The covenant-promise is all-comprehensive. Although it is predominantly a promise of spiritual goods, yet it includes food and drink. Cf. Ps. 111:5, "He hath given *food* unto them that fear him. He will ever be mindful of his covenant." That covenant-promise is "all my salvation and all my desire." II Sam. 23:5. *It is on the ground of this promise that the believer is exhorted not to be anxious about food, drink, and clothing.*

IV. THE DEHORTATION. "BE NOT THEREFORE ANXIOUS FOR THE MORROW; FOR THE MORROW WILL BE ANXIOUS FOR ITSELF. SUFFICIENT UNTO THE DAY IS THE EVIL THEREOF."

The expression "the morrow" indicates "the future." The meaning of "the morrow will be anxious for itself" is *not* that such anxiety is justified. Christ is merely stating a *fact*: even the child of God is often filled with worry because of the difficulties of *today* (the "tomorrow" which has become "today"). Now Christ says, as it were, do not add to those anxieties by worrying about a future which has not yet been realized. The words, "Be not therefore anxious for the morrow," summarize all that has been said. By consulting the two previous Chapters and reviewing this one you will notice that Christ has plainly pointed out that the essence of the righteousness of the Kingdom consists in undivided trust in God over against worry or anxiety. In all, seven reasons have been given why the citizen of the Kingdom should not worry about material things, etc.:

1) Because such anxiety is at bottom materialism; hence, it blinds the eye of the soul to spiritual things, and enslaves the will to Mammon.

2) Because he who created us will certainly provide for us.

3) Because if God, the *Creator*, provides for the birds and robes the lilies; then God, the *Father*, will certainly provide for his children.

4) Because if even animals and plants that cannot "take thought" are provided for, then certainly the children of God who can and should "take thought" for the morrow will receive all they need.

5) Because anxiety will not help any. It is fruitless.

6) Because when "tomorrow" has become "today" there will be sufficient worries.

7) *Because the believer has God's covenant-promise.*

READING AND STUDY HELPS

I refer esp. to G. C. Morgan, *The Gospel According to Matthew*. A popular explanation is found in Ds. J. Van Andel, *Het Evangelie van Lukas*, p. 285 ff., and in J. O. Dykes, *The Relations of the Kingdom*, pp. 47-90. For a study of the covenant-promise permit me to refer to my own little book, *The Covenant of Grace*, price 60 cents, publisher: Wm. B. Eerdmans Pub. Co., 234 Pearl St., N.W., Grand Rapids, Mich.

CHAPTER XXI

THE RIGHTEOUSNESS OF THE KINGDOM
Its Essence With Respect to Our Relation to Man

The Absence of a Censorious Attitude

MATTHEW 7:1-5.
"Judge not, that ye be not judged. For with what judgment ye judge, ye shall be judged: and with what measure ye mete, it shall be measured unto you. And why beholdest thou the mote that is in thy brother's eye, but considerest not the beam that is in thine own eye? Or how wilt thou say to thy brother, Let me cast out the mote out of thine eye; and lo, the beam is in thine own eye? Thou hypocrite, cast out first the beam out of thine own eye; and then shalt thou see clearly to cast out the mote out of thy brother's eye."

I. CONNECTION.

Jesus has pointed out what is the essence of the righteousness of the Kingdom of God with respect to our relation to God. It consists in loving God above all; hence, in the *secret devotion* of the heart to the heavenly Father, Matt. 6:1-18, so that I *give* myself unto him, and in *undivided trust* in God, Matt. 6:19-34, so that I expect to *receive* all things from him.

This having been shown, Jesus now proceeds to indicate what is the essence of the righteousness of the Kingdom with respect to our relation to *man,* to *the neighbor.* He unfolds this theme first negatively; then positively. Negatively, Christ first of all warns against the spirit of censoriousness, springing from the root of self-righteousness. Says he, "Judge not, that ye be not judged." Positively, Christ shows what should be our attitude toward the neighbor. Says he, "All things therefore whatsoever ye would that men should do unto you, even so do ye also unto them: for this is the law and the prophets." That, in brief, is the line of thought which we find in chapter 7:1-12. The detailed development of this train of ideas will become clear as we study this Chapter and the following ones. First the theme mentioned is developed negatively.

II. THE DEHORTATION. "JUDGE NOT."

A. There is a certain connection (though perhaps not a close one) between the last verse of chapter 6 and the first verse of chapter 7. That connection is discovered when one reads the two verses in one breath, "Sufficient unto the day is the *evil* thereof. *Judge not*, that ye be not judged." There is *evil* in the world; physical, but also *moral*: evil thoughts, words, and deeds which we associate with evil men, i. e., with people round about us, for no one is perfect. Now Jesus does not require of us that we should shut our eyes to these evil deeds. On the contrary, the citizens of the kingdom are called upon to counteract them, Matt. 5:13-16.

However, in rebuking the sin of his neighbor the Christian must not follow the example of the Pharisee. He must not in the spirit of self-righteousness condemn others while he forgets the fact that his own moral vision has been seriously impaired by sin. Hence, Jesus says, "Judge not."

B. Meaning: Just what did Jesus mean when he said, "Judge not"? Did he mean that we are not to judge *at all*, i. e., that *all* manner of judging is *absolutely and without qualification* forbidden? But if *that* be the meaning, Jesus and Paul contradict one another. Christ said, "Judge *not* (i. e., do not continue to judge, stop judging); whereas Paul said, "But he that is spiritual judgeth *all things* . . . ." I Cor. 2:15. Nay, if *that* be the meaning, Christ contradicted *himself*. Here he says, "Judge *not;*" in John 7:24 he states, "judge *righteous judgment."* Accordingly, it will not do to ascribe to this passage a crassly literal interpretation. According to sound rules of exegesis and recognized hermeneutical principles the exact meaning of Matt. 7:1 (as well as the exact meaning of all other passages) must be determined from the significance of the *words used in the original,* from the *context,* from *parallel passages,* and from *the general teaching of Scripture* (analogia Scripturae) with respect to the subject under discussion.

In a manner altogether natural, as will be seen, the word used in the original for "judging" has acquired various meanings. These meanings are not so far apart as commonly supposed. Indeed, it is rather easy to trace them to one common origin. The primary significance of the original word seems to be to *separate;*

hence, to *separate in thought,* i. e., to *distinguish* between two or more objects, ideas or propositions, to *discriminate;* consequently, the word has acquired the meaning: to make a choice, to *choose,* to *determine* which of two objects you prefer, to *decide,* to *conclude,* to *determine,* to *resolve,* to *deem.* When you make a choice between two objects, you *select* one; hence, to *select,* to *pick out.* Furthermore, not only to *decide,* but also to *make known your decision,* e. g., to *express an opinion concerning right and wrong: to judge,* to *decree.* This judgment may be either *approbation* or *condemnation;* hence, to *approve,* to *condemn,* as the context may indicate. See Thayer's Lexicon or Young's Concordance for passages which illustrate these various meanings.

The context must determine the exact meaning. Now the connection in which *this* verse (Matt. 7:1) occurs speaks of "beholding the mote that is in the brother's eye but not the beam that is in one's own eye." It is evident, therefore, that the word "judge" is here used in the sense of the term "condemn." This interpretation is supported also by the parallel-passage in Luke, "Be ye *merciful* even as your Father is merciful. And judge not, and ye shall not be judged: *and condemn not, and ye shall not be condemned."*

The meaning, therefore, is, *"Condemn not, i. e., do not judge without mercy, without love;* do not judge *harshly,* in a spirit of *self-righteousness."*

The context indicates that Christ is thinking

particularly of that kind of judging which has for its object *the other person*, never *self*, vss. 4, 5. All *such* judging is condemned.

Now it must be very clear that Jesus does not forbid us to *see the faults of others;* he *wants* us to see them, as is evident from the context, vs. 6; he wants us to *figure* with them also, "Give not that which is holy unto the dogs." Nevertheless, he does not want us to stare ourselves blind upon these faults of others. On the contrary, one of the purposes of seeing the error of the neighbor should always be that we may be the instruments used by God "to convert the sinner from the error of his way," Jas. 5:20; cf. Matt. 7:5b. Moreover, in passing judgment upon another we must always remember that we can do this in a very *relative* sense only, for our own moral vision has been darkened by sin.

It will now be clear that Jesus does not contradict his Matt. 7:1 statement when in John 7:24 he says, "Judge righteous judgment;" Matt. 19:28, "Verily I say unto you that ye . . . shall sit upon the twelve thrones judging the twelve tribes of Israel." Cf. Matt. 18:18; I Cor. 5:12; I Cor. 6:3, etc. Matt. 7:1 speaks of a *self-righteous, loveless, condemnatory* judgment; *that* is forbidden. Matt. 18:18; John 20:23; I Cor. 5:12, 13, refer to the *disciplinary* judgment of the church. *That* is required. Matt. 19:28, I Cor. 6:3, refer to the believers' *participation in the final judgment. That* is promised!

III. THE GROUNDS (REASONS) UPON WHICH IT IS BASED. ". . . . THAT YE BE NOT

JUDGED. FOR WITH WHAT JUDGEMENT YE JUDGE, YE SHALL BE JUDGED. . . . AND WHY BEHOLDEST THOU THE MOTE THAT IS IN THY BROTHER'S EYE, BUT CONSIDEREST NOT THE BEAM THAT IS IN THINE OWN EYE. . . . . ."

A. The unmerciful judge will himself be judged in a similar manner.

1. ". . . . that ye be not judged." According to the original the prohibition, "Judge not," refers to a *habit;* the words, "that ye be not judged," refer to a single (divine) *act.*

2. "For with what judgment ye judge, ye shall be judged, and with what measure ye mete, it shall be measured to you." Meaning: if you judge without mercy, you will be judged without mercy (i. e., by God, though God's *agents* are not excluded, cf. Luke 6:34). You will be condemned by and by. The same thought is repeated for the sake of emphasis. The word "measure" in its primary significance refers to a vessel which holds a certain amount of grain. The man who *loves* his neighbor will give him *good* measure. In turn he will receive *good* measure. So also the individual who having obtained mercy exercises mercy toward his neighbor when he judges him, will receive from God *"a good measure, pressed down, shaken together, and running over,"* Lk. 6:38. The *love* divine which preceded and brought forth this man's love will also in turn answer his love.

B. The unmerciful judge is himself a sinner; hence, he has not the right to condemn others while he is not conscious of his own guilt and pollution. We offer the following translation of the "saying" of Jesus which we are about to study:

"And why do you keep looking at the *chip* in the eye of your brother, while the *beam* in *your own* eye you do not perceive? Or, how will you say to your brother, Hold, I will cast the *chip* out of your eye, and lo, the *beam* in *your own* eye! You hypocrite! *First* cast the *beam* out of your *own* eye, and then you shall see clearly to cast out the *chip* out of the eye of your brother."

The "beam" is a big branch of a tree, a heavy piece of timber fit to be used for the rafter or joist of a building. The "mote" is a "chip" from the beam; it is a little dry twig off the branch.

Just what does Jesus mean? These words have often been interpreted on this fashion: First get rid of your own faults before you criticize others. In other words, to see the faults of others is always wrong, for the time will never come when your own faults have been completely removed. Nevertheless, *that* can hardly be the meaning. Jesus *wants* us to see the errors of others; he wants us to discriminate between brethren and swine, verse 6.

Neither can the meaning be this: First rid yourself of *big* faults (beams); then afterward you can begin to pay attention to the little faults (chips) of your brother. Also on *this* theory we would never be permitted to see the faults of our brother, for who will ever claim that he has "little" faults only? Would not this claim itself constitute a "beam"?

We must look for the meaning of these words in a different direction. Jesus does not rebuke a person because he fails to see that he himself has a *beam;* but he rebukes him because he does not perceive that he has a beam *in his eye,* i. e., that he is *blind; that he cannot see at all; that his own moral perception is completely ruined by his self-righteous attitude and consequent lack of love toward others.* On the other hand, his brother does not claim that he is fit to sit as judge over others. *Comparatively* speaking, we may say (without denying in the least the total blindness of all men by nature) that while the moral vision of the *publican* who *confesses* himself to be a sinner is *impaired,* so that there is a *chip in his eye,* the spiritual perception of the Pharisee is completely *absent.* His self-righteousness renders him *blind.* The Pharisees are "blind guides." Cf. Matt. 23:24, etc. They have a "beam" (self-righteousness with consequent lack of love for others) "in their eye."

If we accept this interpretation, the words of Jesus, "first cast the beam out of your own eye," i. e., first *see* rightly, acquire real meaning. Jesus is not indulging in irony, neither is he requiring the impossible when he makes this demand. He does not ask us to get rid of all our own big faults first before we point out the other man's little errors. He urges us to remove "the beam in our eye," i. e., the attitude of self-righteousness, the "holier-than-thou" disposition, the lack of love for our brother. He wants us to see and constantly confess our own unworthiness and sinfulness so that we may exercise the spirit of forgiving love and mercy toward our brother even when we judge him. This, by grace (not in our own strength) *is possible*.

On the basis of this interpretation the final clause becomes very beautiful. Jesus does not say, "First cast the beam out of your own eye and then *"you will see clearly the chip,"* etc., but he says, *"then shall you see clearly TO CAST IT OUT!"* He wants us to see the "chip" in our brother's eye, but he desires that we shall see it *in order that we may help him to get rid of it*. Only those who have been redeemed by the blood of the Lamb and who have received a spirit of gratitude and humility as a result of Christ's Atonement are able to manifest that spirit. Truly, the Sermon on the Mount can never be *fully* understood apart from the redeeming grace of Christ.

QUESTIONS FOR DISCUSSION. Would you be able to ascribe another person's conduct to jealousy if you did not have the seed of jealousy in your own heart? By accusing another person of jealousy are you, in a measure, condemning yourself? Just what is the meaning of that expression of Paul, so full of depth, " . . . for wherein thou judgest another, thou condemnest thyself," Rom. 2:1. A certain church-member told his pastor that he did not preach enough sermons on *Reprobation*(!). In view of the passage which we have been studying (love, mercy toward the neighbor), what do you think of the attitude of that church-member?

READING AND STUDY HELPS

See the commentaries previously mentioned, esp. G. C. Morgan. Further: articles "Judge," "Judgment," "Beam," etc., in *I. S. B. E.* Commentaries on Rom. 2:1. W. Geesink, *Van 's Heeren Ordinantiën*, IV, p. 396.

CHAPTER XXII

THE RIGHTEOUSNESS OF THE KINGDOM
Its Essence With Respect to Our Relation to Man
Discrimination in Judgment

MATTHEW 7:6.
> "Give not that which is holy unto the dogs, neither cast your pearls before the swine, lest haply they trample them under their feet, and turn and rend you."

I. CONNECTION.

In verses 1-5 Jesus has condemned the Pharisaical attitude of self-righteousness and harshness. *That* point must be well understood. *Not the recognition of faults in others is as such condemned;* but the attitude of the man who condemns others for their dimness of sight, while he himself is totally blind. Whoever lacks *love* is blind. The result of this attitude is that one assumes that between himself and his neighbor there is a great spiritual distance. He says, as it were, "*I* am holy; *he* is a sinner; *I* am justified; *he* stands condemned." Now *that* attitude is wholly wrong. *Yet, on the other hand, we may not close our eyes to the faults of others, even though this implies that seeing their faults we shall see our own.* The progress of God's kingdom and the best interests of the Church of God on earth demand that we heed the admonition of Paul, "Beware of the dogs, beware of the evil workers," Phil. 3:2.

II. MEANING OF THESE WORDS:

A. "Give not that which is holy unto the dogs, neither cast your pearls before the swine . . . ." Notice:

1. The term, "that which is holy," is very general. It signifies whatever has been separated in a special manner unto the service of God. Thus Scripture speaks of holy ground, Ex. 3:5; holy convocation, Ex. 12:16; holy Sabbath, Ex. 16:23; holy nation, Ex. 19:6; a holy place, Ex. 29:31; holy anointing oil, Ex. 30:25; holy linen coat, Lev. 16:4; holy jubilee, Lev. 25:12; holy house, Lev. 27:14; holy field, Lev. 27:21; holy tithe, Lev. 27:30; holy water, Num. 5:17; holy censers, Num. 16:37; holy firstlings, Num. 18:19; holy camp, Deut. 23:14; holy gold, Josh. 6:19; holy bread, I Sam. 21:4; holy ark, II Chron. 35:3; holy seed, Ezra 9:2; holy city, Neh. 11:1; holy covenant, Dan. 11:28; holy word, Ps. 105:42; the sanctuary, Ex. 15:17, with its Holy Place and Holy of holies; holy ones (angels and children of Israel), Deut. 33:2, etc. In all these cases the word holy . . . indicates that the person and objects thus qualified are consecrated unto the Lord and to his service, and that they have been set apart (separated) from the common sphere."[1] Similarly, we today speak about the holy sacraments, the holy offices (of the ministers, elders, and deacons), the holy Sabbath, God's holy house, the holy table of the Lord, the holy Gospel, etc. Now,

Jesus exhorts us not to give that which is holy unto the dogs. The terms "that which is holy" and "pearls" indicate, of course, the same thing(s). Just because a thing has been definitely set aside for God's Kingdom, so that in our minds we at once associate it with God's Kingdom, it may be termed a "pearl" or a "jewel," something which should be considered very precious and should be handled very carefully. Now, Jesus teaches us that we should not give that which is holy to the dogs, neither cast our pearls before the swine. Hence, the question what is meant by:

2. The terms "dogs" and "swine?" In the Orient dogs were held in low esteem. They were the street scavengers, usually homeless and shameless. The worst thing that could happen to a person was that his body should be devoured by dogs, I Kings 14:11; 16:4; 21:19, 23. See further I Sam. 17:43; 24:14; II Sam. 9:8; II Kings 8:13; Isa. 56:10, etc. The Pharisees called the heathen "dogs." Very likely Jesus referred to wicked people who creep into the Church for merely selfish reasons. In Phil. 3:2 and Rev. 22:15 dogs are coupled with evil-workers, sorcerers, etc. If that is the meaning of "dogs," the term "swine" must indicate the same thing. The O. T. mentions the swine as an *unclean* animal, Lev. 11:7; Deut. 14:8. In Isa. 65:4; 66:3, 17, the eating of swine's flesh is called an abomination. Moreover, swine are mentioned in the account of the Gadarene demoniac and in the parable of the prodigal son,

Matt. 8:30 ff.; Lk. 15:15 ff. Dogs and swine are mentioned together in II Pet. 2:22, "The dog turning to his own vomit again, and the sow that has washed to wallow in the mire." From all these references, when carefully studied, the meaning of the passage will become abundantly clear.

3. The expression, "Give not that which is holy to the dogs, neither cast your pearls before the swine," means, accordingly, that Christians are to be very careful whenever it becomes their duty to commit to certain individuals the holy things of God. There are many weak but well-meaning Christians who forget this entirely. Says G. Campbell Morgan, "Do not judge your fellow man hastily; *but when a man has manifested his character, do not give holy things to dogs, do not fling pearls before swine. Remember, if out of false charity or pity you allow men of material ideals . . . to touch holy things . . . presently they will turn and rend you . . . . . There is a separation made within the borders of Christ's Kingdom, and, while we are to indulge in no censorious criticism and final judgment of our fellow man, if that man, judged by his own action and character, is unworthy, then we are not to give him holy things, we are not to cast our pearls before swine.*"[2]

QUESTIONS FOR DISCUSSION. Do we always keep these things in mind? Here is a member of the Christian Reformed Church at whose home there are frequent card parties. She has a way with children, however, and is regarded by some as a possible candidate for Sunday School teacher. Do the words of Jesus apply, namely, "Give not that which is holy unto the dogs, neither cast your pearls before the swine"? There are Christians who advocate open communion. Does the dehortation of Christ apply to that? How does it apply to Passion Plays? Show that it does not apply to mission activity among those who have never heard the Gospel.

B. ". . . . LEST HAPLY THEY TRAMPLE THEM UNDER THEIR FEET, AND TURN AND REND YOU."

Meaning: Swine cannot appreciate the value of pearls. Perhaps they consider them to be beans. Then, noticing that they have not received food, these disappointed brutes will trample upon your pearls, and in their fury may turn and rend you. Similarly, the sin of giving that which is holy unto the dogs will certainly avenge itself upon the guilty individual or the guilty church. The church which entrusts the holy offices to men who are not dependable will soon reap the bitter consequences. It will become a *dead church*. There is no excuse for this grievous sin.

REFERENCES
1) H. BAVINCK, *Gereformeerde Dogmatiek* II, p. 213.
2) G. CAMPBELL MORGAN, *The Gospel According to Matthew*, p. 73 ff.

READING AND STUDY HELPS
H. Bavinck, *Gereformeerde Dogmatiek* II, p. 213 ff. G. Campbell Morgan, *The Gospel According to Matthew*, pp. 73, 74. Articles on "Dogs" and "Swine" in *I. S. B. E.* Article "Hond" in *Chr. Encyclopaedie;* G. M. Mackie, *Bible Manners and Customs*, p. 134.

CHAPTER XXIII

THE RIGHTEOUSNESS OF THE KINGDOM
Its Essence With Respect to Our Relation to Man

Discrimination in Judgment

Wisdom to Judge Aright Obtained by Persevering Prayer

MATTHEW 7:7-11.

"Ask, and it shall be given you; seek, and ye shall find; knock and it shall be opened unto you: for every one that asketh receiveth; and he that seeketh findeth; and to him that knocketh it shall be opened. Or what man is there of you, who, if his son shall ask him for a loaf, will give him a stone; or if he shall ask for a fish, will give him a serpent? If ye then, being evil, know how to give good gifts unto your children, how much more shall your Father who is in heaven give good things to them that ask him?"

I. CONNECTION.

Is there a connection between these verses and the preceding passage? There are many who see no connection at all.[1] According to others Christ returns to the subject of prayer which he had already discussed.[2] Finally, there are those who see a threefold connection.[3]

Although we are aware of this difficulty, we see a logical connection between this passage and the one discussed in the previous Chapter. This is altogether natural. Up to this point we have witnessed a very logical development of

The Sermon on the Mount

ideas, a very easy transition of thoughts. Must we suppose that we are now face to face with a sudden break in the continuity of the sermon? Is this discourse, after all, merely a collection of "sayings of Jesus" uttered at various occasions and under totally different circumstances, and thrown together somehow by one who calls himself Matthew? We beg to differ. In the *preceding* verses Christ has been speaking about our relation to the neighbor, vss. 1-6. In the *succeeding* verse Christ is still speaking about our relation to the neighbor, vs. 12. Is it not altogether reasonable to conclude that the intervening verses (7-11) also deal with an aspect or phase of the subject touching our relation to the neighbor? If this conclusion is warranted, then, in our opinion, the connection is probably as follows:

In the preceding verses Jesus has pointed out that the Christian must beware lest while he is trying to remove the sliver from his brother's eye, he leave untouched the beam in his own eye. Nevertheless, although he should earnestly strive to love all, i. e., to promote every one's good, he must distinguish between *brethren* and *swine*. He must not cast his pearls before the swine. Hence, in a sense he must "judge." Moreover, in view of the fact that all his dealings with the neighbor will be partly determined by this "judgment," Christ requires that he "judge *righteous* judgment," John 7:24. But how will he be able to do this? He cannot "understand the thoughts of his neighbor afar off," and he is not even "acquainted with all his ways." Who will lead, guide, and direct his mind in order that he may not become guilty on the one hand of rashly condemning a *brother* (vss. 1-5) or on the other hand of entrusting "that which is holy" unto a *swine or dog*?

This question Jesus answers by urging the necessity of persevering prayer accompanied by earnest effort, in order that in an *organic way* (e. g., in harmony with the study of and a life according to the Word of God) and in an *ever-increasing measure* God may furnish his children with wisdom to judge aright and to discover the proper relation to each of those with whom they come in contact. Hence, the exhortation, *"ask, and it shall be given to you; seek, and ye shall find"; etc.* To be sure, the exhortation as such is general. It pertains not only to asking for wisdom in *this* matter, but in *all* matters. Nay, it is even broader in its scope and pertains to asking for whatever we need, especially to prayer for the fulfilment of our *spiritual* needs. Hence, the same or a similar exhortation may occur in a different connection. Cf. Lk. 11:1-13. Yet its exact meaning *here* (i. e., in Matthew) is determined in part by the preceding context.

As far as the succeeding context is concerned (with which it is definitely linked by the word "therefore," vs. 12), could anything be more appropriate as an introduction to the command "to treat our neighbor as we like to be treated by him" than *this* advice, namely, to *ask* and to *seek* the Father's assistance in a task which we cannot perform in our own strength?

QUESTIONS FOR DISCUSSION. Whenever a Christian is confronted with the difficulty of distinguishing between a *brother* and a *dog*, he should *ask, seek, knock*. History proves that men totally unworthy of the holy office have at times been allowed to creep into the church just because this advice of Christ was neglected. In this connection, therefore, we wish to refer you to a very valuable question which occurred in Rev. Monsma's Outline on Church Government, *Federation Messenger*, October, 1932, "Is not the calling of a minister . . . worthy of a special prayer service? Should we not go back to this old custom?" We realize, of course, that an answer can be given to this question based on wholly different arguments than the one which we have "suggested."

II. EXHORTATION: ASK, SEEK, KNOCK.

A. ASK:

1. This is the *simplest form* of the command. Notice the rising scale of intensity: ask, *seek*, KNOCK.

2. Asking implies a *consciousness of need*. The Pharisee does not a*sk;* he *tells* the Lord how good he is, Lk. 18:11, 12; the publican *asks*, i. e., *pleads,* "God, be thou merciful to me, a sinner," Lk. 18:13.

3. It also presupposes *belief in a personal God with whom we can have fellowship.* When one *asks*, he *expects an answer;* hence, this implies belief in a God who can, does, and will answer, i. e., in God the *Father.*

B. SEEK:

1. Seeking is *asking plus acting.* Prayer alone is not sufficient. One must be active in endeav-

oring to obtain the fulfilment of his (spiritual) needs; e. g., one should not only *pray* for a deeper knowledge of Scripture, but should also diligently *study* Scripture, attend the services, prepare thoroughly for the meeting of the Bible Class, above all: he should strive to *live* in harmony with Scripture. One should be "zealous" in his striving to obtain spiritual goods. Cf. Chapter XX, II.

QUESTIONS FOR DISCUSSION. As a member of a Bible Class are you "zealous" for the truth; e. g., do you prepare yourself thoroughly at home for the discussion of the lesson? What can you do as an organization to foster greater interest in the study of Scripture on the part of the members of your congregation?

2. Most commentators add something to this effect, "One *seeks* what he has *lost*." Neither the English word "seek" nor the word used in the original necessarily imply this thought, however. Moreover, it is not required by the context.

C. KNOCK:

1. Knocking is *asking plus acting plus persevering*. One knocks again and again until the door is opened. Similarly, one should persevere in the search for wisdom, etc.

2. Knocking also implies that the citizen of the kingdom is conscious of his own inability. He knocks at the door of the kingdom-palace in order that the King, who is at the same time his *Father,* may *give* unto him all the strength which he needs for his own earnest endeavor.

III. THE PROMISE WHICH ACCOMPANIES THIS EXHORTATION.

A. Its Correspondence with the command. The correspondence is *exact: ask* . . . it shall be *given* you; *seek* . . . ye shall *find; knock* . . . . it shall be *opened* unto you.

B. Its Three Lessons. In connection with the exhortation we have here three lessons:

1. *The duty of perseverance* (in prayer and endeavor):

a. According to the original we read, "Continue to ask, to seek, to knock."

b. This idea is emphasized by the threefold form of the command.

c. It is implied especially in the expression, "Keep on *knocking.*"

QUESTION FOR DISCUSSION. Why does not God answer all our prayers *at once?*

2. *The certainty that persevering prayer accompanied with activity will be rewarded:*

a. Notice that in verses 7 and 8 this promise is repeated *six times.*

b. This certainty is based upon an argument from the less to the greater: if even *any earthly* father, who is *evil*, will fulfil the proper desires of his son, then *surely* the *heavenly* Father, who alone is *good*, will answer the prayer of his children!

3. *The promise that God will give us just what we ask, providing what we ask is good for us; hence that he will not always give us exactly what we ask:*

a. The expression "good things" indicates the Holy Spirit and all his benefits (cf. Lk. 11:13): wisdom (cf. previous context), love, etc.

b. If a son asks his father for a cake of bread, the father will give him *that*, and not a white, round stone which resembles it; i. e., he will not *disappoint* him and mock his hunger; again, if the son asks for an eel (fish), the father will give him *that*, and not an eel-resembling serpent; i. e., he will not *deceive* him. Then surely the *heavenly* Father will not disappoint or deceive his children. Bread and fish constituted the two most common articles of food in the Orient. The wise parent will give only *"good gifts"* to his children; so also the heavenly Father will only give us that which will be subservient to our salvation; hence, he will not always give us exactly what we ask. Monica prayed that her son (Augustine) might not go to Italy, for she was sure that Italy would prove his ruin. Yet to Italy he went in spite of (rather: as a result of?) all her prayers, *and there he found Jesus!*

QUESTION FOR DISCUSSION. Was her prayer heard?

REFERENCES

1) H. A. W. MEYER, *Commentary on the N. T., St. Matthew*, vol. I, p. 229. Cf. GROSHEIDE, op. cit., pp. 88, 97.

2) A. T. ROBERTSON, *The Gospel According to Matthew*, p. 114.

3) J. O. DYKES, *The Relations of the Kingdom*, pp. 119, ff.

READING AND STUDY HELPS

In addition to the books already mentioned, see C. G. Chappell, *The Sermon on the Mount*, p. 191 ff. In connection with the subject of *Prayer*, cf. the titles mentioned in chapter XV.

CHAPTER XXIV

THE RIGHTEOUSNESS OF THE KINGDOM
Its Essence With Respect to Our Relation to Man

The Golden Rule

MATTHEW 7:12.
> "All things therefore whatsoever ye would that men should do unto you, even so do ye also unto them: for this is the law and the prophets."

I. INTRODUCTION.

In these words Jesus summarizes his teachings with respect to the proper attitude which the citizen of the kingdom should take toward his neighbors. This attitude was first described negatively, "Judge not that ye be not judged," etc. One should not try to remove the sliver from the brother's eye without an earnest attempt to cast the beam out of one's own eye, vss. 2-5. But although judging in the sense of rash condemnation—a condemnation which is not accompanied by self-accusation—is the object of the Master's severe rebuke, this does not mean that judging in the sense of careful discrimination between "brethren" and "dogs" is also wrong. On the contrary, the citizens of the kingdom must not give that which is holy unto the dogs; they must not cast their pearls before the swine. They must ask for wisdom and guidance in order that they may properly fulfil their moral obligation with respect to each individual neighbor. Their prayer will not be in vain, for "every one that asketh receiveth; and he that seeketh findeth; and to him that knocketh it shall be opened."

But, in order that the Christian may be ready for any emergency, i. e., in order that he may know at any definite moment how to conduct himself toward his neighbor, the Lord now gives a rule which, as it consists of a measuring of one's duty by one's self-love, is "like a pocket-standard, always at hand and prompt of application; of special utility, therefore, in those sudden emergencies which are constantly occurring, in which the child of God is called to act swiftly and alone amid the press of the world's selfish society."[1] This "pocket-standard" is the *Golden Rule*, "All things therefore whatsoever ye would that men should do unto you, even so do ye also unto them: for this is the law and the prophets."

II. HOW DOES THIS RULE DIFFER FROM THE SO-CALLED GOLDEN RULE OF THE MODERNIST?

A. THERE IS A DIFFERENCE. Though there may not be any difference in words, for unbelievers constantly refer to the Golden Rule of Matt. 7:12, yet there must be a difference in *thought,* in *idea.* Modernists of every description regard this rule to be the summary of Christian ethics. We are told at times that this maxim furnishes a common ground upon which the believer and the unbeliever can together rear the palace of peace, good-will, and cooperation. Over against this very generally accepted opinion we shall try to indicate in this Chapter that the *so-called* Golden Rule of the modernist has little if anything at all in common with the *genuinely Golden* Rule which Christ has given us. The two differ in more than one respect.

B. THE GREAT DIFFERENCE DOES NOT CONSIST PRIMARILY IN THIS, THAT CHRIST'S RULE IS POSITIVE WHEREAS NON-CHRISTIAN TEACHERS OF RELIGION HAVE GIVEN US A NEGATIVE RULE. Most commentators—both liberal and orthodox—maintain that Christ's Golden Rule is so much better than the Golden Rule of Confucius and others because while the latter in their maxim have merely told us *what NOT to do, how NOT to act, and how NOT to be disposed* toward our neighbor, Christ, on the contrary, has told us *what to do, how to act, and how to be disposed* toward our fellow-man. Men guided by the light of natural reason have given us a *negative rule* ("wat gij *niet* wilt dat u geschiedt, doe dat ook aan een ander *niet*"), but Christ has given us a *positive rule*. Now in our humble opinion the difference between the negative maxim *as such* and the positive maxim *as such* has been greatly exaggerated. We are willing to admit that as to *form* the positive rule is better because it is more direct. Again, we are willing to grant that with respect to *emphasis* the positive canon is to be preferred. We even concede that in essence the positive rule is much better than the negative *when the latter is interpreted in a very superficial, crassly literal manner:* it certainly is a vastly higher effort of love to shower upon our fellow man every conceivable token of kindness than simply to abstain from any definite act of injury. Finally, we admit without reservation that *CHRIST"S* Golden Rule in its positive form is deeper in meaning than the Golden Rule of *CONFUCIUS* in its negative form; but we add to this the qualification that this difference is not due to the implications of the positive form versus the implications of the negative form, but merely to the infinite difference between the mind of Christ and the mind of Confucius. We do not admit that Confucius was himself fully aware of the meaning and implications of his Golden Rule. It is our contention that the Golden Rule in its negative form, *when considered in its full, deep, comprehensive meaning* is the same in essence as the Golden Rule in its positive form. When you say, "Do *not* do unto others what you would *not* like to have them do unto you," do you *necessarily* mean only this: do not *kill* your neighbors; do not *steal* their property; do not *slander* their good name. etc.? Our answer is a definite *No*. You mean much more. In a word you mean: *do not treat your neighbors with anything less than genuine love, for you would not like to have them treat you with anything less than genuine love.* Hence, *when considered in its full, deep meaning*, the negative rule is identical in essence to the positive rule. Hence, we do not fully agree with the statement of Dykes, ". . . . this negative form of the rule falls immensely beneath the positive . . . ."[2]) We answer, "Not necessarily." Jesus emphatically teaches that the law with its *negative* commandments (thou shalt *not* kill; thou shalt *not* commit adultery; thou shalt *not* forswear thyself) is fulfilled in the application of the *positive* rule, "Thou shalt *love* the Lord thy God with all thy heart, etc., and thou shalt *love* thy neighbor as thyself," Matt. 5:21 ff.; 5:27 ff.; 5:33 ff.; 5:43 ff.; 19:19; 22:37 ff. The *sum and substance,* i. e., *the fulfillment* of the O. T. law which consisted in *negative* commandments, is the *positive* command to *love.* Cf. the expression, "for this IS the law and the prophets." The negative implies the positive. Our Heid. Catechism in its interpretation of the Ten Commandments takes the same view. Moreover, Rom. 13:9 is conclusive on this point. We read, "For this, Thou shalt *not* commit adultery, Thou shalt *not* kill, Thou shalt *not* steal, Thou shalt *not* covet, and if there be any other commandment, it is *summed up* in this word, namely, Thou shalt *love* thy neighbor as thyself." It is indeed strange that this fact, so plainly taught in Scripture, has escaped most commentators.

QUESTIONS FOR DISCUSSION. There are those who claim that it is wrong to send missionaries to China, seeing that we would not welcome Chinese missionaries (Confucianists, Buddhists) to our country. Is this a proper application of the Golden Rule? Why not?

The evident meaning of the Golden Rule is this: as you desire that your neighbor shall *love* you, so you also should *love* him.

C. THE GREAT DIFFERENCE (BETWEEN CHRIST'S GENUINELY GOLDEN RULE AND THE SO-CALLED GOLDEN RULE OF THE MODERNIST) CONSISTS FIRST OF ALL IN THIS: CHRIST'S GOLDEN RULE PRESUPPOSES A DIFFERENT ENABLING POWER. The non-Christian religious prophet of yesterday and the one of today view the Golden Rule (in whichever form) as a *requirement which man is able to fulfil in his own strength; the believer confesses the contrary to be true.* The unregenerate man believes in the moral (as well as physical) evolution of the race; he looks forward to the complete actualization of "the kingdom of God" on earth; to a time when, as a result of a lengthy process of training in man-centered religion, men will at last have reached the summit of the mountain of holiness and love. Scripture, however, paints a different picture with a view to the future. It tells us that men shall be *"lovers of self . . . without natural affection, implacable . . ."* and that by nature they are even now *"living in malice and envy, hateful, hating one another,"* II Tim. 3:2; Tit. 3:3. Man of himself is not able to *live* the Golden Rule. He needs *"the washing of regeneration and renewing of the Holy Spirit,"* Tit. 3:5. Unbelievers (in varying degrees) are guided by a different rule. It is this, "Whatsoever *men do to you, even so do ye also unto them.*" This is the law of *revenge.*

D. THE GREAT DIFFERENCE CONSISTS SECONDLY IN THIS: CHRIST'S GOLDEN RULE HAS A DIFFERENT SETTING OR BACKGROUND. The modernist severs this rule of love toward *man* from the commandment of love toward *God*. According to his view the Golden Rule is the sum and substance of all ethics. The one "big" thing in life is service to our fellow man. It is in support of this contention that religious liberalism will appeal to Christ's Golden Rule. But it has no right to do this; for in the Sermon on the Mount the Golden Rule is preceded by a lengthy discourse in which Jesus teaches us to love *God above all*. This implies the inner devotion of the heart to God, Matt. 6:1-18, an undivided trust or confidence in the Father, Matt. 6:19-34. Now it is in the light of that love toward God the Father that we, as children of the heavenly Father, are taught to love our neighbor who was created in God's image, Matt. 7:1-12. To be sure, the Golden Rule of the modernist resembles Christ's Golden Rule. Its music is the same in *pitch*, but not in *quality*, just as a note when played on the piano differs very much in quality from the same note played on an organ. The entire instrument behind the note, i. e., the entire background is different.

E. THE GREAT DIFFERENCE CONSISTS FINALLY IN THIS: CHRIST'S GOLDEN RULE IS DIFFERENT IN PURPOSE; HENCE, IN ESSENCE. Fully stated, the *so-called* Golden Rule of the modernist would generally read somewhat as follows, "All things therefore whatsoever ye would that men should do unto you, even so do ye also unto them, *for in the end this will pay*." It is the best *policy;* just as honesty is the best *policy*. *The gold of the modernist's rule is,* to a large extent, *fool's gold.* It merely glitters. It is the pyrite of utilitarianism.

QUESTION FOR DISCUSSION. Is the so-called Golden Rule of the modernists *mere* selfishness or is it in part the result of "the glimmerings of natural light, whereby man . . . discovers some regard for virtue, good order in society, and for maintaining an orderly external deportment"? Cf. "The Canons of Dort, III and IV, article 4.

Christ's Golden Rule is wholly different. It is, "All things therefore whatsoever ye would that men should do unto you, even so do ye also unto them, *for this is the law and the prophets.*" That is: do this *not because in the end it pays, but because God says so in his law, i. e., in the O. T. ("law and prophets") and in the N. T. And GOD IS SOVEREIGN.* Notice, moreover, the word *"therefore"* with which Christ's Golden Rule is linked with the preceding. Says Christ, *". . . . how much more shall your Father . . . give good things to them that ask him. THEREFORE, i. e., out of gratitude for what the Father has given to you, and in order that you as children may resemble your Father, THEREFORE you should love your neighbors even as you desire that they love you, in order that the stream of love toward the undeserving beginning in heaven may flow on and on, not only to your hearts, but also through and from your hearts until it reaches even the most wicked neighbor. This, indeed,—and this ONLY—is the GOLDEN RULE.*

QUESTION FOR DISCUSSION. Did Christ practice the Golden Rule?

The Sermon on the Mount

REFERENCES
1) J. O. DYKES, *The Relations of the Kingdom*, p. 144.
2) Same, p. 141. Here, for once, we differ with Dykes and with most commentators.

READING AND STUDY HELPS

We realize that the view given above is so different from that ordinarily presented that it is difficult to point to many sources for further study. In our opinion most commentaries fail to do justice to this passage. We might refer for additional reading to J. Stalker, *The Ethic of Jesus*, p. 291 ff.; W. Geesink, *Gereformeerde Ethiek*, I, pp. 401, 412, 433. Here Geesink makes the statement, "Het door Jezus uitgesproken beginsel der reciprociteit is echter niet specifiek christelijk, maar algemeen menschelijk." He refers it to the gratia communis. Do you wholly agree? Further, p. 466; II, 32. G. C. Morgan, in the *Gospel According to Matthew*, shares the common view that the great difference between the Golden Rule of Confucius and that of Christ consists in the difference between the negative and the positive form. He calls this a "radical difference." Cf. p. 75 ff.

CHAPTER XXV

EXHORTATION TO ENTER THE KINGDOM
The Beginning of the Way:
The Narrow Gate and the Straitened Way versus the Wide Gate and the Broad Way

MATTHEW 7:13, 14.
> "Enter ye in by the narrow gate: for wide is the gate, and broad is the way, that leadeth to destruction, and many are they that enter in thereby. For narrow is the gate, and straitened the way, that leadeth unto life, and few are they that find it." Cf. Luke 13:24.

I. CONNECTION.

With this passage we begin the explanation of the last main division of the Sermon on the Mount. Christ has told us who are the citizens of the kingdom, Matt. 5:1-16. Next, he has described at length the righteousness (the fundamental law, the constitution) of the kingdom, Matt. 5:17-7:12. In this third or final section of his great discourse he urges us to enter into the kingdom, Matt. 7:13-7:27. When we employ the term "enter" with reference to this entire section, we are using it in its broadest sense; in a sense every bit of progress which the Christian makes on the path of sanctification is a new entrance into the kingdom of God. In the passage which we are studying, Matthew 7:13, 14, the term "enter" is used in a more restricted sense. It refers to the beginning of conscious spiritual life, when one "enters in by the narrow gate." In due order Christ in this section pictures the *beginning* of the Christian's path, verses 13, 14; gives warnings with reference to his *progress* upon this path, verses 15-20; and finally contrasts the *end or issue* of the path of the Christian with the issue of the path of the unbeliever, verses 21-27.

II. INTERPRETATION OF THIS PASSAGE CONSIDERED AS A WHOLE.

A. THE PASSAGE SHOULD BE VIEWED AS A UNIT. The interpretations of this passage are many. One is liable to become confused when he considers all the various explanations, some of which are in direct contrast with others. If we are not entirely mistaken, the cause of this confusion is the fact that many commentators see only the various parts or elements of this beautiful saying of Christ, but fail to view the passage as a unit. It is our conviction that we shall never arrive at a true insight into the meaning of this admonition as long as we see nothing else than the two gates, the two ways, the two kinds of travellers, and the two destinations. As a result of this purely analytical treatment two problems have arisen which would not have presented themselves if justice had been done to the unity of the passage:

B. THE FIRST PROBLEM WHICH HAS ARISEN BECAUSE THE UNITY OF THE PASSAGE WAS FORGOTTEN. Does Christ mean, "Enter ye in by the narrow gate *in spite of the fact* that it is narrow," as seems to be the view of some of the older commentators; or does he mean just the opposite, namely, "Enter ye in by the narrow gate *because* it is narrow; choose the straitened way *because* it is straitened"? There is the dilemma. Which horn do you choose? Personally, we choose neither one. Our answer is: Jesus does not teach in this passage that men should enter in by the narrow gate *in spite of the fact* that it is narrow, neither does he teach that they should enter in by the narrow gate *because* it is narrow; *but he teaches that we should enter in by the narrow gate because it is the narrow gate which admits to the way of LIFE; and he invites us to tread the straitened path because it is this path which leads to LIFE.* Only this interpretation does justice to the unity of the entire passage.

C. THE SECOND PROBLEM WHICH HAS ARISEN BECAUSE THE UNITY OF THE PASSAGE WAS LOST SIGHT OF. This is closely related to the first. Those commentators who tell us that Christ meant that men should enter in by the narrow gate *in spite of the fact* that it is narrow, are usually also of the opinion that Christ pictures the path of the Christian as full of gloom and difficulty, as not a bit rosy, as only dark and dismal. They will emphasize the fact that Jesus calls the gate "narrow," the way "straitened," and that these terms refer to the Christian's afflictions, self-denials, and sufferings. Some seem to conclude that the *Christian's way is wholly dark and dismal in contrast with the road which the unbeliever travels which is wholly agreeable.* But this view does not seem to harmonize at all with the eight-fold "Blessed" by means of which Christ has described the felicity of the Christian at the very beginning of this sermon; neither does it harmonize at all with various other passages in Scripture, e. g., Ps. 1 (the contrast seems to be just the opposite here); Ps. 7:10; 9:1-6; 13:5; 16:8, 9; 18:12; 18:32 ff.; 21:1 ff.; 23; 27:1; 30:1 ff.; 32:1 ff.; 33:1 ff.; 34:1 ff.; 37:3 ff.; 37:25 ff.; 45:1 ff.; 46:1 ff.; 47:1 ff., etc.; Is. 57:21 cf. with 59:8; I Cor. 2:9, 10; I Cor. 3:21*b*; Eph. 1:3 ff.; Phil. 3:1; 4:10 ff., etc., etc. In all these passages the life of the Christian is described as the life of joy, of peace, of comfort, of blessing.

Hence, it should not surprise us at all when we find that many other commentators have adopted a view which is the exact opposite of the first. They tell us that the terms "narrow gate" and "straitened way" point to the *safety and security* of the Christian; to the fact that the Christian is protected by God's grace and love. Moreover, they inform us that the broad way is the *busy way;* and the busier the road (the greater the traffic), the greater will also be the number of dangers and accidents; while on the narrow path there is hardly any room for an accident. Summing up, therefore, their contention is that Jesus bids men to enter in by the narrow gate and to travel on the straitened way *because the path of the Christian is wholly safe and secure.*

Again, we refuse to accept either of these interpretations. The words used in the original for "narrow" and "straitened" seem to militate against the second view. Both of these words are often used to suggest affliction, self-denial, hardship, effort.

The first word "narrow" is STENĒ. Just to aid your memory think of the Dutch word *steunen*, German *stöhnen*. Its meaning is: narrow, strait. It is sometimes used metaphorically to indicate that which is *close, cribbed, confined*. In combination with another word it means *distress, anguish*, Rom. 2:9; 8:35; II Cor. 6:4; 12:10.

The second word "straitened" is TETHLIMENNĒ. It is derived from a root which is often used in Scripture to denote *pressure, affliction, distress, tribulation*. Cf. Matt. 24:9; Acts 7:11; 11:19; Rom. 12:12; II Cor. 1:4, 8; 4:17; 6:4; 7:4; 8:2; II Thess. 1:6; Rev. 1:9; 2:9, 22; 7:14, etc.

It is interesting to observe that in Rom. 2:9 we have these same two words used side by side (i. e., we have the same roots). There we read THLIPSIS KAI STENOCHŌRIA. The English rendering is *"tribulation and anguish."* Cf. also Rom. 8:35 and Trench, *N. T. Synonyms*, par. 55. It is altogether probable, therefore, that when Jesus speaks of the gate as being *narrow* and of the way as being *straitened*, he is thinking of the difficult aspect of the Christian life. See further under III, A and B. *The way of the CROSS leads home! That is apparently the idea of the entire passage.* Blessed are ye when men shall reproach and persecute you! See the Chapter on that passage which also states the reason why these are called blessed, i. e., why it is the narrow gate and the straitened way that lead unto life. Says Meyer, "*Wide* gate and *broad* way are figures which represent the pleasures and excesses of sin and wickedness. *Strait* gate and *narrow* way represent, on the other hand, the effort and self-denial which Christian duty imposes."[1]

Does this mean that the former of the two interpretations of this passage is correct? It does not. For, although the path of the Christian is one of *affliction, self-denial, effort, and suffering,* this does not mean that it is wholly dark and dismal. In the midst of his suffering for the Master's sake the Christian experiences in his heart the peace of God which passeth all understanding. He has joy unspeakable and full of glory. He "*greatly rejoices, though now for a little while he is put to grief in manifold trials.*" Cf. Paul's phrase, "as sorrowful, *yet always rejoicing.*" In the midst of his afflictions the Christian rejoices because of the work which God has done for him, is doing for him, will do for him and for all that love Christ's appearing. He rejoices because he knows that "the sufferings of this present time are not worthy to be compared with the glory which shall be revealed to us-ward." He rejoices even more when he considers that "our light affliction, which is for the moment worketh for us more and more exceedingly an eternal weight of glory." Hence, subjectively the *burden* of affliction becomes lighter and lighter in comparison with this increasing weight of comfort, peace, and glory. It becomes easier to bear. The path of Christian *blessedness* "forever grows broader until at last it becomes broad in the fulness of eternal life."[2] Nevertheless, the gate and the path of *affliction* remain *narrow and straitened*. And we are urged to enter in by the narrow gate and to travel on the straitened way not *because* they are narrow and straitened, neither *in spite of the fact* that they are narrow and straitened, *but because they lead unto life*. This interpretation, it would seem to us, does justice to the unity of the entire passage and avoids extreme views.

III. INTERPRETATION OF THE ELEMENTS OF THIS PASSAGE.

A. THE TWO GATES.

Notice that these gates are not at the end of the road, but at the beginning. Jesus mentions first the gate, then the way. The "gate" is the entrance portal and the "way" is the path to which it admits. *Gate* and *way* together lead to the court of the stately dwelling. Hence, the narrow gate does not mean the gate of heaven at the end of our life on earth. It must, therefore, represent the *beginning* of conscious Christian life, i. e., *conversion*. To be sure, by means of *regeneration* one enters the kingdom of heaven, John 3:3-5, etc., but regeneration is wholly God's work; it cannot be enjoined. Christ here issues a command, "Enter." Hence, the gate must mean conversion rather than regeneration. *The narrow gate is the conscious choice to serve God; this gate is narrow, indeed.* It *means strenuous EFFORT. It means that we must by God's grace and through his strength strip ourselves of all SELF-RIGHTEOUSNESS, etc. It means persecution. The wide gate is the conscious choice of the world with all its pleasures.*

B. THE TWO WAYS.

The broad way is called "broad" because 1) *those who walk upon it follow their own inclinations; they do as they like, and* think *that this is liberty;* 2) *it is so alluring at first;* 3) *it is the "busy" road, i. e., "many are they that enter in thereby." The narrow way is called thus because* 1) *the thoughts, words, and actions of those who travel it must all conform to God's holy law as the rule of gratitude, to the righteousness of the kingdom: loving God above all and the neighbor as oneself, this makes the road very narrow, indeed; moreover, it is the way of humiliation and of affliction; of the loss of all selfrighteousness and of complete reliance upon God; it is the way of grace;* 2) *it is a way which* in the beginning and to the proud man *does not seem very inviting;* 3) *there are only "few who find it."*

QUESTION FOR DISCUSSION. How do you harmonize this statement of Christ with Rev. 7:9?

C. THE TWO KINDS OF TRAVELERS.

Those who choose the wide gate and the broad way are called "many"; those who enter in by the narrow gate and travel the straitened road are called "few."

QUESTION FOR DISCUSSION. In L. Boettner's work, *The Reformed Doctrine of Predestination*, a book which has been very highly recommended, we read that "the saved shall far outnumber the lost;" that "much the larger portion of the human race has been elected to life;" that "all of those dying in infancy are among the elect;" and that the text which we are discussing, Matt. 7:14, in which we read that those who find the way of life are "few" merely "describes the conditions which Jesus and His disciples saw existing in Palestine in their day," etc. What do you think of these statements? Prove your answer.[3])

D. THE TWO DESTINATIONS.

The broad way leads to destruction, a destruction which begins even in this life (to live apart from thee is DEATH), is continued in an aggravated form after soul and body separate, and reaches its climax after the Judgment Day. The straitened way leads to life, a life which in principle is enjoyed even here on earth, John 5:25, 26; *which refers here to conscious enjoyment and experience of the believer's mystical union with Christ* (remember the figure: the gate is first; then the way) *and which is everlasting and ever-increasing,* John 3:16; 10:10; II Cor. 3:18; Matt. 25:46, etc.

REFERENCES

1) H. A. W. MEYER, *Commentary on the N. T.*, Part I, Vol. I, p. 231.

2) G. CAMPBELL MORGAN, *The Gospel According to Matthew*, p. 77.

3) L. BOETTNER, *The Reformed Doctrine of Predestination*, pp. 138, 139, 149.

READING AND STUDY HELPS

In addition to the various works and commentaries mentioned in previous Outlines, read W. Parks, *The Five Points of Calvinism*, pp. 20-56; H. Bavinck, op. cit., II, p. 410 ff.; A. Hodge, *The Atonement;* C. Bouma, *Geen Algemeene Verzoening;* L. Boettner, *The Reformed Doctrine of Predestination*, esp. pp. 136-149. This book is very valuable. Nevertheless, its universalistic tendency, remarks on infant salvation, discussion of supra and infralapsarianism, do not entirely satisfy us. C. G. Chappell, *The Sermon on the Mount*, pp. 204-216; A. Maclaren, *Exposition of Holy Scriptures* on Matt. 7:13, 14. You find a very interesting interpretation of this passage in Dr. G. Brillenburg Wurth's book *De Bergrede en Onze Tijd*, pp. 36, 37. According to him the "broad" way is the way of obedience to the law as a means toward salvation. It was the way advocated by the Pharisees. The "narrow" way is the way of grace"; cf. our own explanation.

CHAPTER XXVI

EXHORTATION TO ENTER THE KINGDOM
Warning with Respect to the Christian's Progress Upon the Way:

False Prophets Who Lead Many Astray

MATTHEW 7:15-20.
"Beware of false prophets, who come to you in sheep's clothing, but inwardly are ravening wolves. By their fruits ye shall know them. Do men gather grapes of thorns, or figs of thistles? Even so every good tree bringeth forth good fruit; but the corrupt tree bringeth forth evil fruit. A good tree cannot bring forth evil fruit, neither can a corrupt tree bring forth good fruit. Every tree that bringeth not forth good fruit is hewn down, and cast into the fire. Therefore by their fruits ye shall know them."

I. INTRODUCTION.

Not only is an admonition necessary with respect to the *beginning* of the path, but also with respect to one's *progress* upon it. To be sure, when a man is once on the right path, he can never be lost, John 10:27, 28; yet this does not mean that the Christian is kept on the right way by outward compulsion. By means of warnings, admonitions, afflictions, etc., etc., God keeps his children on the way which leads to ever-increasing life. Hence, in our passage the Lord warns us against false prophets, who come to us in sheep's clothing, but inwardly are ravening wolves.

In this connection we should study what Jesus

has said concerning these false prophets in his discourse concerning the last things, Matt. 24, 25; Mk. 13; Luke 21. The warning, moreover, is a very timely one. It should be heeded today as well as when Christ first spoke these words. We are living in a very peculiar age; in an age of instability, of inconstancy, of unsteadiness of religious views. To be sure, there always have been religious currents and cross-currents ever since the days of Christ's sojourn on earth; and even in his days there were various religious parties; such as the Essenes, the Pharisees, and the Sadducees; but what has been a fact in the past is much more a fact today. Today the religious atmosphere is simply surcharged with the lies of the false prophets. We are at the center of a veritable cyclone of contrary doctrines. We are in danger of becoming engulfed by a veritable deluge of false prophecy, and unless we maintain keen vigilance and heed the admonition of Jesus, we shall soon be ensnared in a labyrinth of cults and sects, isms and schisms, denominations and (of late also) undenominations, from which there will be no escape.

II. THE FALSE PROPHETS: THEIR CHARACTER AND MANNER OF APPEARANCE.

"Beware of false prophets, who come to you in sheep's clothing, but inwardly are ravening wolves."

1. General characteristics of false prophets. We shall give these in a way which you can easily store in your memory. The prophets in-

dicated are *fanatic, false, foolish;* they *fulminate* their errors in every conceivable manner, and they bring forth bad *fruits* by which you can know them.

2. They are *fanatic*, i. e., they are characterized by extravagant zeal and they usually try to concentrate your attention upon one point of truth or error at the expense of everything else. Usually upon their pet theory of salvation, e. g., The House of David: "Never shave or fall in love"; Russellism, "Scorn the devil's scholars and get ready for the millennium." K. K. Klan, "Pay ten dollars, get exalted, and save America for God."[1] The very enthusiasm with which these theories are being promulgated is sufficient evidence for the fact that their authors, the false prophets of today, are fanatic. Cf. e. g., the "religious" fanaticism of the atheists in Russia.

3. They are *foolish*. If space allowed, we would point out some of the glaring inconsistencies inherent in Russelism, Christian Science, Spiritualism, etc. As space is very limited, we shall confine our remarks to Mormonism. The Mormons (Church of Jesus Christ of Latter Day Saints!) believe that their book of Mormon was copied and translated from Golden Plates deposited in the hill Cumorah, and written upon by an angel from heaven. Yet any cursory reading of the first editions of the Book of Mormon—corrections were made in later editions—will convince one that this "inspired document" has no respect whatever for the rules of gram-

mar. Cf. e. g., these sentences, "He went forth among the people, waving the rent of his garment, that all might see the writing that he had wrote upon the rent." "Ammon and his brethren saw the work of destruction among those who they so dearly beloved, and among those who had so dearly beloved them." "The number of the slain was not numbered because of the greatness of their number." "Yea, if my days could have been in them days, but behold I am consigned that these are my days." According to this same "inspired" book God once ordered a certain Jared to make barges in which to cross the ocean. Upon completion (they were made exactly as God had ordered) they were found to be airtight. When the people complained, God answered that in order to get fresh air they should make a hole in the top of these boats *"and in the bottom thereof."* A hole *in the bottom of a boat* for fresh air!

4. They *fulminate* their errors in every conceivable manner. Their agents will call on you. Their voices are often heard over the radio. Their missionaries go everywhere seeking to proselytize. At the death of Pastor Russell as many as twelve million copies of his books had been either sold or given away. Rutherford's books have been given away in even greater numbers.

5. They are *false*. That is the characteristic mentioned in our passage. Our passage pictures them as coming in sheep's clothing, but inwardly being ravening wolves. In Rev. 13:11 they

are pictured as having horns like a lamb, but speech like a dragon. Both descriptions mean this: everything that meets the eye, the outward appearance, is appealing; but inwardly, really, essentially (for speech is the expression of the inner thought) these prophets are wolves, dragons, i. e., they are satanic. In them the devil appears as an angel of light.

SUBJECT FOR DISCUSSION. Show that this is true in regard to the Russellites; the prophets of modernism; the Mormons; the leaders of Christian Science, etc.

By calling them ravening wolves Christ emphasizes their desire to destroy the Church.

III. HOW WE MAY KNOW THEM. *"By their fruits ye shall know them. . . Every good tree bringeth forth good fruit, but the corrupt tree bringeth forth corrupt fruit."*

1. The meaning, in brief, is this: we should examine the fruits (i. e., the life, the works, but in this case especially the *doctrine and teachings*) of these prophets by the light of the Word of God; specifically: we should see whether their teachings harmonize with the Sermon on the Mount and with all of Christ's discourses. If the prophet—which, in this connection does not necessarily mean one who predicts the future, but simply a religious teacher—brings forth good fruit, i. e., if his teachings harmonize with those of God's Word, then he is a true prophet, for the good tree brings forth good fruit; if not, he is a false prophet.

2. Judged by this standard, it is easy to see that the Russellites are false prophets, which is

also true with respect to the Mormons, the Spiritualists, the prophets of Christian Science, the Humanists, etc.

SUBJECT FOR DISCUSSION. Show that this is actually the case with respect to all of these.

3. "Do men gather grapes of thorns, or figs of thistles?" It is possible that Christ is here referring to the fact that fruits resembling grapes grow on certain thorns; *but they are not real grapes;* while fruits resembling figs, when seen from a distance, grow on certain thistles; *but they are not real figs.* So also a false prophet does not preach the true doctrine. To be sure, he may do so for a time. But in the end, if we closely watch him, his life, his works, especially his teachings, we shall be able to detect that he is indeed a false prophet.

IV. THEIR END. *"Every tree that bringeth not forth good fruit is hewn down and cast into the fire."*

The Judgment Day, followed by eternal perdition, awaits the false prophet.

REFERENCES
1) Taken from C. W. FERGUSON, *The Confusion of Tongues.*

READING AND STUDY HELPS
In addition to the regular commentaries, read the following works in connection with the study of the false prophets: J. K. Van Baalen, *Our Birthright and the Mess of Meat,* a book which should be in every library. On the different isms see the titles mentioned in that book. C. W. Ferguson, *The Confusion of Tongues,* a book which one should read with discretion.

CHAPTER XXVII

EXHORTATION TO ENTER THE KINGDOM
The End of the Way
Sayers versus Doers

MATTHEW 7:21-23.
> "Not every one that saith unto me, Lord, Lord, shall enter into the kingdom of heaven; but he that doeth the will of my Father who is in heaven. Many will say to me in that day, Lord, Lord, did we not prophesy by thy name, and by thy name cast out demons, and by thy name do many mighty works? And then will I profess unto them, I never knew you: depart from me, ye that work iniquity."

I. CONNECTION.

We have reached the beginning of the final paragraph of the Sermon on the Mount. This final paragraph is very clearly connected with the preceding passage. In *that* passage Jesus warned against *false prophets*. In *this* paragraph Jesus is still speaking about false prophets, who will say, "Lord, Lord, did we not *prophesy* by thy name," etc.

Nevertheless, we notice a slight difference between the thought of the former paragraph and the idea of this passage. Whereas in verses 15-20 Christ viewed these prophets as false because they try to deceive *others* (hence the warning, "By their fruits ye shall know them"); in verses 21-23 he points out that they are false also in this sense: that they deceive *themselves*.

They will expect to enter, but will not be able. Moreover, whereas in verses 15-20 Christ was speaking of (false) *prophets* only, in verses 21-23 his remarks are not confined to them, as is evident from verse 21, "Not every one that saith unto me, Lord, Lord, shall enter into the kingdom of heaven." Self-deception is a sin of which not only prophets are guilty.

Again, we notice a definite progress in the discourse. Whereas in verse 13 Christ was thinking especially of the *beginning* of the way of life, and pictured the "gate" by which he urges men to enter as located at the *entrance* of the way (not at the *end* of the way), in verses 21-23 he is speaking of the *end* or *issue* of the way: he definitely refers to final entrance into the "kingdom of heaven" in *"that* day." This progress in thought as well as the growing solemnity of the final paragraph clearly point to the fact that our Lord's discourse is bending to its close.

Finally, it is interesting to observe that this final paragraph is subdivided into two parts. In verses 21-23 Christ speaks of *"sayers* versus doers"; in verses 24-27 he refers to *"hearers* versus doers."

II. THE LAW OF ENTRANCE INTO THE KINGDOM OF HEAVEN.

A. This Law Stated Negatively, *"NOT every one that saith unto me, Lord, Lord, shall enter into the kingdom of heaven."*

1. This passage implies that even at this time people called Jesus, "Lord, Lord." A difficulty

presents itself here. According to Grosheide and others the expression "Lord, Lord," as we find it here, is simply a polite form of address.[1] When the Greeks came to Philip, they said, *"Sir,* we would see Jesus," John 12:21. They used the same word which has been translated "Lord" in our passage. If that is the meaning here also, then we might translate as follows, "Not every one of those who are calling me Sir, Sir, shall enter into the kingdom of heaven." As proof that this was really all that Jesus had in mind, we are reminded of the fact that at this early stage of the Lord's ministry the disciples did not yet know him in the fulness of his sovereign Lordship. That knowledge came gradually. Cf. Matthew 16:13-16. Moreover, an appeal is also made to I Cor. 12:3, *"no man can say, Jesus is Lord, but in the Holy Spirit,"* but the disciples had not yet received the Holy Spirit (i. e., not in the sense in which they received the Holy Spirit on the day of Pentecost). On the other hand, Machen in his excellent work, *The Origin of Paul's Religion,* sees in our passage a reference to Christ's absolute Lordship.[2] In our opinion we must keep in mind, on the one hand, that the full implications of Christ's sovereign Lordship were not yet seen by the disciples. Nevertheless, on the other hand, we should not forget that many amazing miracles had preceded the Sermon on the Mount. The opinion of many even at this early stage of Christ's ministry may be gathered from such statements as the following: Mk. 1:27,

"And they were all amazed, insomuch that they questioned among themselves, saying, What is this? a new teaching! with *authority* he commandeth even the unclean spirits, and they obey him. And the report of him went out straightway everywhere. . . ." Mk. 1:45, "And they came to him from every quarter." Mk. 2:12, ". . . . they were all amazed, and glorified God, saying, We never saw it on this fashion." John 1:49, "Nathanael answered him, Rabbi, thou art the Son of God; thou art the King of Israel." Cf. Matt. 4:23—5:1; Lk. 4:36, 37; 4:43, 44; 5:26, etc. It is therefore *possible* that in the case of some of those who addressed Christ the words, "Kurie, Kurie," implied more than a mere polite form of address. Moreover, in verse 22, "Many will say to me in *that day*, Lord, Lord," the expression, "Lord, Lord," certainly means more than "Sir, Sir." In the Judgment Day many will *pretend* to recognize in Christ their *Sovereign*. Finally, the parallel passage which we find in Lk. 6:46 certainly seems to imply that the term "Lord" as used here and in Matt. 7:21, 22 is more than a polite form of address. We read in Luke, "And why call ye me *Lord, Lord, and do not the things which I say?*"[3] Accordingly, although we are ready to grant the debatable nature of this question, yet, on the basis of the arguments which we have presented it would seem to us that when Jesus says, "Not every one that saith unto me Lord, Lord, shall enter into the kingdom of heaven," he means at least this, "Not every one who keeps on recognizing me with the lips as his *master*, i. e., as the One who has *authority* over him, shall enter into the kingdom of heaven."

2. Jesus wants men to address him as "Lord, Lord," but he does not want them to do this *and nothing else*. He wants them to *mean* it, and to show in their lives that they *mean* it, by earnestly endeavoring to obey Christ's commands out of gratitude.

3. The term "kingdom of heaven" as used here refers to the kingdom in perfection: the redeemed universe of the future, the new heaven and earth in which will dwell righteousness. The fact that Christ refers to the kingdom in its future manifestation is evident from the reference to the Judgment Day, verse 22. Cf. Chapter II, B, 2—especially II, B, 2 (*c*), 4, and (*d*).

B. THIS LAW STATED POSITIVELY, *"But he (shall enter into the kingdom of heaven) that doeth the will of my Father who is in heaven."*

1. The "kingdom of heaven" is the realm in which God's *will* or *sovereignty* is recognized and cheerfully acknowledged. Hence, "he that doeth the *will* of my Father" will enter the kingdom of heaven. In the second part of the Sermon on the Mount Christ has explained what is the *will* of the Father.

QUESTION FOR DISCUSSION. Why do we say that God's *Sovereignty* is the fundamental principle of the Christian religion?

According to the original we read, ". . . . . he that continues to do the will," etc.

The Sermon on the Mount

2. Just what does Jesus mean when he says, "*my* Father"? In which sense does he call himself, by inference, the Son of God? In the same sense in which we can all call God our Father? Matt. 6:9; 7:11, etc. In answer to these questions we call your attention first of all to the fact that *Jesus does not call himself a son of God in the same sense in which we are sons of God. Christ's sonship is altogether unique; it is different from ours; hence, in order to indicate this difference between his own sonship and ours, Christ generally uses the term "my Father" when he refers to the former, and the term "your Father" when he is thinking of the latter;* cf. Matt. 11:27, Matt. 6:8. The next question is: in which way is Christ's sonship altogether different from ours? Only in *degree*, or in *essence?* In other words, when Jesus calls God *"my Father"* in distinction from *"your Father,"* does he merely mean that whereas we know God and trust in him and have communion with him *to some extent, he* has *perfect* knowledge of God and communion with him? Does Jesus merely teach his own perfect *ethical sonship* (a relation of most intimate knowledge, communion, love); or does he teach this *and more*, i. e., does he perhaps call God his Father because he enjoys community of *essence* with the Father? The latter appears certainly to be the case, e. g., in Matt. 11:25-28; Matt. 14:33 (Jesus apparently accepted the testimony of the disciples); John 1:18; 3:16, etc., where Jesus is called the "only begotten Son"; John 5:18 where

Jesus calls God "his *own* Father," etc. Now if, as has been proved, Christ was conscious of his *natural, essential, divine or trinitarian* sonship, then is it not altogether reasonable to believe that whenever Christ used the term "my Father" a reference, direct or indirect, to this *divine sonship* was never wholly excluded? Cf. the following passages: Matt. 7:21; 10:32; 11:27; 12:50; 15:13; 16:17; 18:10; 18:19; 20:23; 24:36; 25:34; 26:39; 26:42, 53; Lk. 10:22; 22:29; 24:49; John 5:17, 18, 43; 6:32; 8:19, 28, 38, 49, 54; 10:17, 18, 29, 30, 32, 37; 12:26; 14:7, 12, 20, 21, 28; 15:1, 8, 10, 15, 23, 24; 16:10; 18:11; 20:17. To be sure, Jesus was God's Son in a fourfold sense: (1) in an ethical, moral, or religious sense: in the sense that he was a "child of God"; (2) in an official sense, as being the Messiah; (3) in a nativistic sense, i. e., God was in a sense the Father of his human nature; and (4) in the trinitarian sense, i. e., the Father eternally generates him; accordingly, he partakes of the divine *essence*, and is the Son of God *by nature. But these four are not completely separated. In the case of* Christ *the first three rest upon the fourth.*

3. For the expression "Father who is in heaven" see Chapter XV, III.

III. THE EXECUTION OF THIS LAW.

A. THOSE WHO ARE AFFECTED BY ITS PROHIBITION: *false prophets, etc. "Many will say to me in that day, Lord, Lord, did we not prophesy by thy name, and by thy name cast our demons, and by thy name do many mighty works?"*

1. Think of Judas, Demas, the sons of Sceva, etc. Cf. Matt. 24:5, 24, etc. In all probability we should not think of three different groups: false prophets, exorcists, and wonder-workers, but of one group, as would seem to be evident from the wording.

2. "Did we not prophesy, etc., *by thy name?*" This does not mean "at thy command," but has reference to the fact that these false prophets or teachers of religion would point to Christ as the source of their doctrines and of their miracle-working power.

3. ".... in *that day.*" This term indicates the day in which God's majesty will reveal itself; it refers in the final analysis to the Judgment Day.

QUESTIONS FOR DISCUSSION. Premillennialists tell us that there can be no "general judgment" for all men, but that Scripture plainly teaches three[4], four[5], five[6], six[7], or seven[8]) judgments. In the light of the following texts what do you think of their assertion: Is. 2:11, 17; Jer. 30:7; Mal. 3:2; 4:1; Job 21:30; Zeph. 1:14-16; Matt. 7:22; 10:15; 11:22; 12:36; 16:27; Luke 10:12; John 6:39, 40, 44, 54; 11:24; 12:48; Rom. 2:5; I Cor. 3:13; 4:5; II Cor. 5:10; II Tim. 4:1, 8; II Peter 2:9; I John 4:17; Rev. 6:17, etc. Do these passages teach *one* judgment day or *half a dozen* judgments or judgment days?

B. THE MANNER IN WHICH IT WILL BE EXECUTED. "*And then will I profess unto them, I never knew you: depart from me, ye that work iniquity.*"

1. Notice the words, "And then will *I* profess unto them. *I* never knew you; depart from *ME*," etc. These words must have filled his hearers with amazement, for here Jesus reveals that HE HIMSELF is the Judge. Says Gibson, "We can

well imagine that from this point on to the end there must have been a light in his face, a fire in his eye, a solemnity in his tone, a grandeur in his very attitude, which struck the multitude with amazement, especially at the *authority* (verse 29) with which he spoke."[9]

2. The term "profess" indicates an open declaration heard by all in the Judgment Day.

3. *"I never knew you."* "Never," i. e., not a single moment. Just what does Jesus mean when he says, "I never *knew* you"? There is a knowledge of the *mind;* there is also a knowledge of the *heart.* As far as the former is concerned, Christ, the Judge, is omniscient, i. e., he knows all things. Mentally he has known these false prophets to perfection. It is *just because* he has *"known"* them so thoroughly that he is able to judge them. But there is also a knowledge of the *heart,* i. e., of *mutual love,* of *friendship,* of *communion.* Says Paul, *"But if any man LOVETH God, the same is known by him,"* I Cor. 8:3. Cf. Gal. 4:9; I Cor. 13:12; II Tim. 2:19; Am. 3:2. Especially Nahum 1:7*b*, ". . . . he *knoweth* them that take refuge in him"; John 10:14*b*, "I *know* mine own, and mine own *know* me." The connection makes plain the meaning in our passage: the false prophets speak as if Jesus had been their friend. They say, "Did we not prophesy by thy name," etc. Jesus replies, as it were, "As *friends* I have not known you for even a single moment." Cf. Lk. 13:25-27.

4. *"Depart from me."* They will depart forever from the physical presence of the Judge,

and they will never abide in the loving presence of God. Hence, their punishment consists in "eternal destruction *from* the face of the Lord and *from* the glory of his might," II Thess. 1:9. The "departure" spoken of indicates a removal into the place where "there shall be the weeping and the gnashing of the teeth," Lk. 13:27, 28. This punishment will be "everlasting," Matt. 25:46, etc. Yet, just as heaven will be heaven for God's children because *God* is there (i. e., with his *loving* presence) even so hell will be hell for the false prophets, etc., because *God* is there (i. e., with his presence of *wrath*). Cf. Ps. 139:1-12. God is *everywhere-present.* But he is not present everywhere in the same sense.

5. ". . . . *ye that work iniquity."* Literally, ". . . . ye that work *lawlessness* (that which is contrary to God's law). Their great sin was that although they had known the *law* of the kingdom, they had not walked accordingly.

6. Notice the contrast. *They* had boasted that they had performed so many *good* works, e. g., "mighty works in thy name, casting out demons," etc. Jesus, however, calls these men *workers of lawlessness.* Does not this statement imply that Christ regarded their so-called "good works" to be "works of lawlessness," i. e., evil works? This introduces us to some very interesting problems in connection with the "good" which the unbeliever can do. May we be permitted to urge you to exercise the utmost caution in your study of this rather difficult subject? Do not jump at conclusions.

QUESTIONS FOR DISCUSSION:

1. Just how would Christ answer the question: Can unbelievers do good works? Cf. Matt. 7:17-23; Mk. 7:21-23; 10:18; Lk. 6:43; 13:1-5; 18:9-14; 18:19; John 3:3-5; 5:24, 25.

2. What is the prevailing representation of Scripture in regard to this subject? Be sure to study each of the following passages: Gen. 6:5; 8:21; Ps. 51:5; Jer. 13:23; 17:9; Ezek. 36:26; John 1:5; Acts 26:18; Rom. 3:10-18; 6:17, 20; 8:5-8; 14:23; I Cor. 2:14; Eph. 2:1-5; 4:17-19; 5:8; Col. 2:13; Tit. 3:3-5; Jas. 3:11; I Pet. 4:3.

3. How do you harmonize with the passages referred to under 2 the following: II Kings 10:29-31 (cf. Hos. 1:4); 12:2, 3; Lk. 6:33; Rom. 2:14; and Matt. 7:11?

4. When a few passages of Scripture *seem* to differ from the general teaching of Scripture, should we then interpret the few in the light of the many, or the many in the light of the few?

5. Do you agree with this statement: "The unregenerate can do *natural, civil, and religious good*, but he cannot do *spiritual good?*" We are not expressing an opinion; merely offering a question for discussion.

6. Theologians speak of *natural good* (eating and drinking; sleeping and taking exercise); *civil good* (also called civic righteousness: honesty in business; in general: a regard for virtue); *religious good* (such deeds which are religious in a merely *outward* sense, e. g., attending church); and *spiritual good* (which proceeds from faith, etc.). Would you regard natural, civic, religious, and spiritual good as so many branches growing from the same stem, i. e., would you co-ordinate them? Are they different only in degree?

7. Do the "virtues" of the heathen *please* God? Does Rom. 8:8 apply here?

8. It is maintained: (a) that man is totally depraved, *wholly* incapable of doing *any* good and inclined to *all* wickedness, unless he be *regenerated* by the Spirit of God; (b) that the unregenerate, nevertheless, perform many deeds which we should admire, which put us to shame, etc.; and (c) that the solution lies in the fact that these admirable virtues or acts are wholly due to the *general operation* of the Holy Spirit and his influence upon the heart of the unregenerate. Do you consider this a real solution? Does it *remove* the problem or does it merely *move* the problem?

8. According to our confessions just what are good deeds? Cf. Q. and A. 91 of the H. C.

10. Is man by nature *wholly* incapable of doing *any* good, and inclined to *all* wickedness?

11. Is it not true that Scripture itself in a very few instances uses the term "good" in a more general, i. e., external sense? Cf. Lk. 6:33. If Scripture does it, then can any one deny us the right to use the term in that relative sense, providing we use every caution and do not emphasize that which Scripture does not emphasize?

12. Does one speak the *whole* truth when he calls the virtues of the heathen *splendid vices* or *glittering sins*? Must we not admit that the virtues of the heathen are relatively better than their vices?

13. Criticize this statement, "Something is good or it is evil, not relatively, but absolutely." Is it not true that even the very best deeds of believers are, in a certain sense, only *relatively* good, i. e., they are *"imperfect and polluted with sins"*? On the other hand, is it not true that between the *least sinful* deed of the unregenerate and the *most imperfect* good deed of the regenerate there is a gulf which can never be bridged?

REFERENCES

[1] GROSHEIDE, op. cit., p. 93.

[2] J. G. MACHEN, *The Origin of Paul's Religion*, p. 295 ff.

[3] Says Ds. J. VAN ANDEL in *Het Evangelie van Lukas*, p. 144, "Uit dat woord blijkt *dat Jezus reeds door velen uit het volk als Heer erkend werd.*"

[4] H. BURTON, *The Three Judgments*.

[5] W. E. BLACKSTONE, *Jesus is Coming*, p. 103.

[6] C. LARKIN, *The Spirit World*, p. 144. You find the same view in *Dispensational Truth*. Also in C. I. SCOFIELD, *Rightly Dividing the Word of Truth*, p. 42.

[7] C. I. SCOFIELD, *Rightly Dividing the Word of Truth*, note on p. 9; cf. p. 42.

[8] C. I. SCOFIELD, *Reference Bible*, p. 1351.

[9] J. M. GIBSON, *The Gospel of St. Matthew*, p. 722 in Vol. IV of The Expositor's Bible.

READING AND STUDY HELPS

1. On the meaning of the word "Lord" (*Kurios*) see J. G. Machen, *The Origin of Paul's Religion*, pp. 293 ff.; Boussett, *Jesus der Herr;* G. Vos, *The Princeton Theo-*

logical Review, XV, pp. 21-89, 1917; H. C. Sheldon, *The Mystery Religions and the New Testament*, p. 87 ff.; R. J. Knowling, *The Testimony of Paul to Christ;* Article "Lord" in *I. S. B. E.*; A. Kuyper, Sr., *Pro Rege*, I, pp. 342, 344, 348; H. Bavinck, *Gereformeerde Dogmatiek*, II, p. 135 ff.; K. Dijk, article "Heer, Heere," in *Chr. Encyclopaedie*.

2. On God's Sovereignty see especially H. Meeter, *The Fundamental Principle of Calvinism*.

3. On Christ's Sonship I know of nothing better than G. Vos, *The Self-Disclosure of Jesus*, esp. pp. 140-228. Cf. G. B. Stevens, *The Theology of the N. T.*, p. 54 ff.

4. In regard to the question relative to "good works" on the part of the unregenerate, study H. Bavinck, op. cit., III, p. 118; IV, p. 276; W. Parks, *The Five Points of Calvinism*, pp. 1-19; A. Kuyper, Sr., discusses this problem (completely to your satisfaction?) in *De Gem. Gratie*, II, p. 13 ff. See further H. Kuiper, *Calvin on Common Grace*, esp. p. 230 ff. You will find a defense of the *Third Point* (cf. Acts of Synod, 1924, p. 146), relative to civic righteousness on the part of unbelievers, in L. Berkhof, *De Drie Punten in Alle Deelen Gereformeerd*, p. 49 ff.; and an attack on the position of Synod in H. Hoeksema, *A Triple Breach in the Foundation of the Reformed Truth*, esp. pp. 67-87. Before answering the Questions for Discussion would it not be well to read and study all this material thoroughly, especially the Scriptural passages to which we have referred, and also our Confessions, etc., e. g., *Belgic Confession*, Artt. XIV, XV; *Canons of Dort*, III, IV; *Heidelberg Catechism*, Q. and A. 5, 7, 9, 62, 87, esp. 91 and 114; *Compendium*, Q. and A. 7, 12, 46, 65, 66, esp. 68?

5. In connection with the Judgment Day, see the works mentioned under References. Also: any good work on Reformed Dogmatics, e. g., Bavinck or Berkhof. Also: C. E. Brown, *The Hope of His Coming*, p. 243 ff.; W. H. Rutgers, *Pre-millennialism in America;* Y. P. De Jong, *De Komende Christus*.

NOTE: *There is sufficient material in this chapter for at least two meetings. Our advice: Do not try to cover the entire chapter in one evening.*

CHAPTER XXVIII

EXHORTATION TO ENTER THE KINGDOM
The End of the Way:
Hearers versus Doers

MATTHEW 7:24-29.
"Every one therefore that heareth these words of mine, and doeth them, shall be likened unto a wise man, who built his house upon the rock: and the rain descended, and the floods came, and the winds blew, and beat upon that house; and it fell not: for it was founded upon the rock. And everyone that heareth these words of mine, and doeth them not, shall be likened unto a foolish man, who built his house upon the sand: and the rain descended, and the floods came, and the winds blew, and smote upon that house; and it fell: and great was the fall thereof.

And it came to pass, when Jesus had finished these words, the multitudes were astonished at his teaching: for he taught them as one having authority, and not as their scribes."

Cf. LUKE 6:46-49.
"And why call ye me, Lord, Lord, and do not the things which I say? Every one that cometh unto me, and heareth my words, and doeth them, I will show you to whom he is like: he is like a man building a house, who digged and went deep, and laid a foundation upon the rock: and when the flood arose, the stream brake against that house, and could not shake it: because it had been well builded. But he that heareth, and doeth not, is like a man that built a house upon the earth without a foundation; against which the stream brake, and straightway it fell in; and the ruin of that house was great."

I. CONNECTION.

These verses constitute the sublime close of this most wonderful discourse. The entire parable of the Two Builders is connected with the preceding passage by the word "therefore." The transition is about as follows: Those that do not really *carry out* the will of the Father will by and by have to listen to these terrible words, spoken to them: "Depart from me, ye that work iniquity." Therefore, i. e., seeing that all their *speaking about* Christ and *mere listening to Christ* has not resulted in *deeds for* Christ, and was not accompanied by real *loving knowledge of Christ*, but has made their punishment so much the heavier—in view of the fact that while knowing the way they did not walk it—*therefore* these people are *fools*. They have worked hard; they have labored and built; *but they have built upon the sand, and not upon the real foundation.* Anyone who does that is foolish. Those, on the other hand, who *not only say* many things about the Christ and the way of salvation, and *not only hear* the message of salvation, i. e., the Gospel of the Kingdom, *but also obey this message* are *wise:* they have been blessed with wisdom from above. *They have built upon the true foundation.*

This final passage is connected with the entire discourse, as is evident from the fact that Jesus refers to "these words of mine," i. e., the whole sermon.

The great lesson contained in this closing passage is this: he only is a Christian who earnestly endeavors to OBEY Christ. It is the same lesson which we find, e. g., in the Parable of the Four Kinds of Soil, Mark 4:1-20. Notice especially verse 20, "And those are they that were sown upon the good ground; *such as HEAR* the word, and *ACCEPT* it, and *BEAR FRUIT*, thirtyfold, sixtyfold, and a hundredfold." Cf. Jas. 1:22a.

QUESTIONS FOR DISCUSSION. Some stress the religion of the HEART (emotionalism); others, of the HEAD (intellectualism); still others, of the HAND (activism). Does Jesus in this parable of the Two Builders reject the first two and endorse the third? Or, does the word "DO" as here used refer to more than outward deeds? According to the teachings of Jesus should our religion be primarily a religion of the HEART, or of the HEAD, or of the HAND? Study Mark 12:28-31.

II. THE TWO BUILDERS. *"Every one therefore that heareth these words of mine, and doeth them, shall be likened unto a wise man, who built his house upon the rock, i. e., who digged and went deep, and laid a foundation upon the rock . . . And every one that heareth these words of mine, and doeth them not, shall be likened unto a foolish man, who built his house upon the sand, i. e., who built a house upon the earth without a foundation."*

A. Notice, first of all, that in *this* paragraph Jesus is speaking only about those who *hear* the Gospel. Both of the builders are *hearers*.

B. *All* hearers are builders. Strictly speaking there is no neutrality in religion. When one hears the Gospel, he never remains exactly the same person he was before. Even his seeming *indifference* is in reality a positive *hardening* of the heart against the influences of the Gospel. Says Chappel beautifully, "We are building all the time, whether wisely or foolishly. We are building by everything that we do. We are building by every thought that we think. We are building by every word that we speak, every dream that we dream, every picture that we hang upon the walls of our imagination, every ambition that we cherish."[1] The "house" is the sum-total of our thoughts, words, deeds, etc. The house is our life. What we *teach* is *certainly* included. Cf. previous context. In the Judgment Day (and even before, but *then* publicly) God will either *speak well* of our house or he will *condemn* it. Every thought, word, and deed has its *after-effects;* this is true even in regard to the sin which has been *forgiven:* the person who was converted soon after he took the poison, and whose sin was *forgiven,* nevertheless *dies.* Study II Sam. 12:13, 14 in this connection. Moreover, "God will bring *every work* into judgment, with *every hidden thing, whether it be good, or whether it be evil,"* Eccl. 12:14. Finally, the degree of our reward will be measured out to us *according to our works.*

C. The great question is not whether you are a builder (for we *all* are), but whether as a builder you are *wise* or *foolish.* The *wise* man is the one who chooses the best goal and the best means to realize that goal. In *our* passage the exact meaning, viewed in the light of the entire context, seems to be that the *wise* man is the man who has *foresight,* who is *sensible,*[2] who *has an eye for the future;* the *foolish* man is the one who is thinking only of the present.

The *wise* man, spiritually, is the one who by the grace of God builds the palace of his life upon *the foundation;* so that when the storms of life come, the house will remain standing.

D. Notice the *antithesis,* the *fundamental contrast.* Jesus does not speak about four or five builders; but about *two* builders. He constantly divides men into *two* classes. Cf. Matt. 5:13, 14; 6:22, 23; 7:13, 14; 7:17, 18; 7:21-23; 7:24-27; 10:16; 10:39; 11:25, 2(?); 13:11, 12; 13:14-16; 19-23 (good ground versus ground that is *not* good, though for various reasons); 13:24-30; 13:36-43; 13:47-50; 22:1-14; 25:2, etc.

QUESTION FOR DISCUSSION. It has been claimed that the theory according to which in the ethical sense all men constitute one great family, so that all men are brethren, and God is the Father of all men FINDS ITS SUPPORT ESPECIALLY IN THE SERMON ON THE MOUNT. Make a study of the texts referred to, and PROVE THAT THE OPPOSITE IS THE CASE: IN THIS VERY SERMON (AS WELL AS ELSEWHERE) JESUS STRESSES THE ANTITHESIS!

E. Notice the figure Jesus uses. There were two men. Each built a house. The "houses" to which Jesus refers were probably constructed of a few unhewn stones, daubed with untempered mortar, while the roof was of earth and grass. Cf. Ps. 129:6; Mk. 2:4. The houses themselves were not strongly built; hence, everything depended upon the *foundation.* Now, according to this figure, both of these houses were erected in a valley containing the bed of a water-course. During the "dry season" in the Orient the riverbed is dry or nearly so. Both houses stand equally well. But what will happen when the rainy and stormy season comes? Then everything will depend upon the foundation. Now, the one builder, lacking all foresight, has erected his house upon the loose gravel of the valley. The other builder first removed this loose gravel; he "digged and went deep," i. e., down to the rock under the drift sand, and there he laid a *foundation*. According to the words of Jesus the man who builds his house upon the rock is a picture of the individual who not only *hears* the Gospel of the Kingdom, the proclamation of the *will* of the Father, but who also *acts upon* it, realizing that his life will have abiding value only then when it is built upon *the solid foundation of* THE DOING OF GOD'S WILL, THE JOYFUL RECOGNITION OF GOD'S SOVEREIGNTY. *That* is the "foundation" or "rock" (for, whether we do so *directly* or *indirectly* we shall have to give a spiritual meaning to this "foundation"). Inasmuch as *in Christ we see the very personification of this principle,* John 4:34, and furthermore whereas *it remains forever impossible for us to do God's will, to recognize him and obey him as our Sovereign* in our own strength, and because *we can do this only by means of the power merited for us and given to us by Christ;* hence, we can say that in the last analysis *the Rock, the Foundation is* CHRIST. Is. 28:16; Rom. 9:33; I Pet. 2:6; I Cor. 3:11.

On the other hand, the builder who erected his house upon the sand indicates the person who, although he knows the way of salvation,

The Sermon on the Mount 245

refuses to think of the future; he refuses to remember that he "has but one life; 'twill soon be past; only what is done for Christ will *last*"; hence, he is a *hearer,* but not a *doer;* he follows the promptings of his own sinful will, and refuses to obey and recognize God as his *Sovereign,* i. e., he does not build upon the Rock, *Christ.*

III. THE TEST TO WHICH THEIR BUILDINGS ARE SUBJECTED. ". . . . *and the rain descended, and the floods came (arose), and the winds blew, and beat upon (smote upon) that house, and the stream brake against that house."*

A. Picture the scene. A day of testing comes. Notice that it comes for *both* houses. Says Dykes, "One of those terrific storms of rain and hail which the treacherous winds of the Levant bring up suddenly from the sea, swells the brook in a few hours into a torrent; and when the flood sweeps down its narrow channel like a tide, turbid and white with foam from one rocky bank to the other, while the fierce rainstorm drives up the ravine before the western gale, and lashes on roof and sides, then is put to proof the stability of both dwellings; then everything depends upon the character of their foundation."[3]

B. So also for every hearer of the Gospel, whether he be a *doer* or not, the test is surely coming. It comes in various forms: in the form of *trial,* Gen. 22:1, Bk. of Job; of *temptation,* Gen. 39:7-18; Mk. 14:53-72; of *bereavement,* Gen. 42:36; Job. 1:18-22; Lk. 7:11-17; of *sick-*

ness, Is. 38; Matt. 8:5-13; 9:18-26; John 11:1 ff.; of *prosperity,* Mk. 10:17-31; of *death;* and finally, of *the judgment in the last Day,* Heb. 9:27; Matt. 25:31 ff. We do not agree with those who limit the meaning of the "tempest" to *death.* The *all-decisive* moment may come long before death.

QUESTIONS FOR DISCUSSION. Just what is the difference between God's PROVING and Satan's TEMPTING? Is it true that Satan always TEMPTS a man when God PROVES him? Why is it that, according to all appearances, one individual is tested much more severely than another? Is this true even with respect to Christians? Why? Just what is the difference between the important lesson which Jesus teaches in this parable, and the lesson contained in I Cor. 3:10-15?

IV. THE OUTCOME OF THE TEST. ". . . . *it,* (i. e., the house which was built upon the rock) *fell not; was not even shaken.* . . *It* (i. e., the house which was built upon the sand) *fell or fell in; and great was the fall thereof: the ruin of that house was great."*

A. When the floods come and beat against the house built upon the rock, they may indeed lay bare the walls of this house to the very rocks, the *foundation holds: the rock is not removed by the waves and the winds. Hence, the house is not even shaken.* Notice the play on words; literally, "The winds blew and *fell* against that house . . . . but it *fell* not." On the other hand, when these same waters break against the house which has no foundation at all, they carry away the very gravel upon which the house was erected; they undermine the walls, and reduce the house to *utter ruin*. The contrast becomes even more striking when we notice the fact that according to the original the winds *"fell against"* the house built upon the rock, i. e., they beat against that house *with all their destructive energy;* yet *that* house stood solid, it "fell not"; while these winds merely *"stumbled against"* the house built upon the sand, and with a sudden and great crash it fell. The house built upon the rock held out against all the violence of the terrific storm; it withstood every furious onslaught of the wind; it braved every tumultous torrent of rain. When the force of the storm was completely spent .. . there stood the house, none the worse for the storm! On the other hand, the other house fell as soon as the wind merely *stumbled against* it (not "against its foundation," Lenski, for it *had no foundation: that* is exactly the point). It was blown over like a house of cards.

B. Notice that according to Luke the one man has built his house upon a *foundation*. The other built his house *without a foundation*. Luke does not say: on a *weak* foundation, but *without any foundation*. Either the fundamental principle of your life is the cheerful recognition of *GOD'S SOVEREIGNTY, THE DOING OF GOD'S WILL THROUGH THE GRACE OF GOD AND OUT OF GRATITUDE,* so that you are building on the Rock *Christ,* John 4:34; or your house (i. e., your life) *has no foundation at all.* In *that* case when the storms of life descend upon the structure of your life, when death comes, and especially when the Judgment Day dawns, there will be a *crash*, *"then shreds of wreckage upon the raging waters, and the ruin will be complete. For other foundation can no man lay than that is laid, which is Jesus Christ."*[4]

V. CONCLUSION. *"And it came to pass when Jesus had finished these words, the multitudes were astonished at his teaching: for he taught them as one having authority, and not as their scribes."*

Throughout the sermon or discourse Christ had shown his authority, for *a)* He did not rely on human sources like the scribes, but said, "Verily *I* say unto you," (Matt. 5:18, 20, etc.; *b)* He spoke *the truth*, for he *was* (and *is*) *the truth*, John 14:6; and *c)* He revealed himself as *the Coming Judge, before whom shall be gathered all the nations*, Matt. 7:22, 23; cf. 25:31.

The Sermon on the Mount ends in the manner in which it began, i. e., by emphasizing the one fundamental principle of Christianity, the very *essence* and the *root-idea* of the "kingdom of God," namely, *obedience to the will of God, joyful recognition of God's SOVEREIGNTY. May we all be "doers" of God's will and not "hearers" only!*

QUESTION FOR DISCUSSION. What is the Roman Catholic interpretation of the S. on the Mt.? The Lutheran? That of Karl Barth? The Premillennialistic? The Ritschlian? The eschatological? See Dr. G. Brillenburgh Wurth's *De Bergrede en Onze Tijd*, pp. 8-27.

REFERENCES

1) C. G. CHAPPELL, *The Sermon on the Mount*, pp. 218, 219.

2) E. J. GOODSPEED, *The New Testament, An American Translation.*

3) J. O. DYKES, *The Relations of the Kingdom*, p. 205.

4) C. G. CHAPPELL, op. cit., p. 226.

READING AND STUDY HELPS

Study the commentaries on Matthew, Luke, and on The Sermon on the Mount which were mentioned in the preceding chapters. Also the following articles in *I. S. B. E.*: "House," "Build," "Building," "Builder," "Foundation," "Rock," "Sand," "Temptation." Lenski has a beautiful paragraph on the "authority" with which Christ preached. Be sure to compare our interpretation of the Kingdom of God and of the Sermon on the Mount with that of Ritschl, that of A. Schweitzer (in *The Mystery of the Kingdom of God*), and that of J. Weiss (cf. Das Reiches Gottes). By all means read Dr. G. Brillenburg Wurth's *De Bergrede en Onze Tijd* and Dr. A. M. Brouwer's *De Bergrede.*

APPENDIX

Matt. 5:32. According to most translations the husband *makes his wife an adulteress* by divorcing her. We shall furnish proof.

Here are some of the versions with which we are most familiar:

"But I say unto you, That whosoever shall put away his wife, saving for the cause of fornication, *causeth her to commit adultery.*" (A. V.)

" . . . *makes her an adulteress.*" (A. R. V. and Moffat.)

" . . . *makes her commit adultery.*" (Goodspeed.)

" . . . *die maakt dat zij overspel doet.*" (Dutch Staten Vertaling.)

" . . . *der macht dass sie die Ehe bricht.*" (German.)

Most commentators agree with this translation. Witness, e. g., the following remarks on this verse:

"To commit adultery," i. e., to violate her marriage vow against her will by forced separation or compulsory deserton. Or the words may have prospective reference to the case mentioned in the last clause, that of re-marriage on the part of the repudiated wife who thereby violates the vow by her own act, but by the procurement if not under coercion of her husband." Thus Alexander.

"The clause implies the circumstance that after divorce the woman will be likely to marry again. . . . If a man divorces his wife *he causes her to commit adultery* (it being presupposed that she will remarry) because ideally her first marriage still holds good. If a man marries such a divorced woman, he not only causes her to commit adultery, but himself does so, since he marries one who ideally is still the wife of her first husband." Thus W. C. Allen in the *I. C. C.*

" . . . causeth her to commit adultery, — viz., by contracting another marriage, strictly speaking, the actual adultery consists in and dates from the remarriage of the woman who had been divorced . . . the husband who divorces his wife is morally the cause of *her committing adultery*, and in that respect even more culpable than she." Thus J. P. Lange.

These are but a few "samples."

On the surface, even apart from further study, this translation is rather difficult to accept. According to it, whenever a husband wantonly breaks his marriage vow and divorces his wife, even though she has not committed adultery, *she* becomes an adulteress. Some, of course, at once add that her adultery is merely of a formal character, i. e., the fact as such that she is not living with her husband constitutes adultery. *Sinless adultery on her part, therefore!* Others again emphasize that although she becomes an adulteress by the act of her husband, yet *he* is mainly to blame. She becomes an adulteress because *he made her an adulteress*. But that explanation leaves her an adulteress, a great sinner! Just why? What has she done? She has become an adulteress merely because her husband divorced her. This explanation sounds about as logical as it would be to say that a man becomes a thief because his property is stolen, and he becomes a murderer because he was murdered!

But there is a third subterfuge to which the advocates of this translation will at times resort. We are told that the meaning is not that she becomes an adulteress when her husband divorces her, but when she marries *another man*. We do not deny that Jesus may have used these words with a "prospective reference" to what immediately follows. We ask, however, did Jesus actually say that the woman *becomes* (or, *is made*) an *adulteress? The fact is that Jesus is not discussing the sin (if any) of the woman at all, but as is evident from the entire context, he is speaking about the sin of the husband! Not she is an adulteress, but he is an adulterer. That* is the point!

When we consider everything, it seems to us much more probable that we have here a *wrong translation to begin with*. As far as the first part of this passage is concerned we consider the translation given by Dr. H. Bouwman, Grosheide, Lenski, Thayer, Zahn, to be far more accurate. However, when Lenski in his excellent commentary remarks that "Zahn alone sees that the infinitive is passive," and that "dictionaries, commentaries, and translators treat *MOICHEUTHĒNAI*, and then, of course, also *MOICHATAI*, as active," he is making a too sweeping statement. Although by far the majority of commentators are guilty of this error, this is by no means true of all. Lenski is in very good company. Bouwman translates (or *interprets*), "De man, die zijn vrouw wegzendt, is oorzaak dat *zij overspel ondergaat*" (Art. "Echtscheiding" in *Chr. Encyclopaedie*). Grosheide has, "Die maakt dat *zij overspel lijdt.*" Thayer in *Greek-English Lexicon of the N. T.* has this under *MOICHEUO*, "passive of the wife, *to suffer adultery, be debauched:* Matt. 5:32a." Lenski himself has, " . . . brings about that *she is stigmatized as adulterous.*"

In general, we agree with these translations. It is difficult, of course, to determine the exact shade of meaning, and it is perhaps even more difficult to give a translation which will "sound" well in English. We prefer the rendering given by Thayer, Bouwman, Grosheide, as being a more exact translation than that given by Lenski. The woman who is released by her husband *suffers* adultery. She is not merely *stigmatized* as an adulteress. It is very difficult if not impossible to determine conclusively whether Jesus had reference merely to the fact that she suffers the shame and disgrace of having been divorced by her husband as well as the hardship of having to face the struggle of life alone, and the temptations that are in store for her, or whether the words have a "prospective reference to a future marriage," which is possible also on *our* interpretation. In that case (and in view of the immediately following clause this interpretation is certainly possible) the translation "causes her to *be debauched*" is perhaps better. The meaning then is that she is "led astray morally" when she consents to marry another, seeing that in the eyes of God the first marriage still stands. But even if that be the meaning, Christ is not speaking of this marriage to another from the aspect of *her* guilt, but he is definitely thinking of the guilt of her *husband* (in the first part of the passage) and of the *man* who marries the divorced wife (in the second clause). Jesus is not referring to *her* adultery, but to *her husband's adultery.* She *suffers* wrong. He *does* wrong. It is even possible that Christ is thinking both of her present embarrassment and of her future marriage. *One* thing is clear: she *suffers* adultery.

The reasons why we accept this translation and why we have made a plea for the passivity of the verb (in the first part of the passage) are as follows:

a. The verb is definitely *passive* in form. It is *MOICHEUTHĒNAI*. This is the passive aorist infinitive. We see no good reason why a *passive* should be translated as an *active*.

b. The verb is not only *definitively* passive, but it is *purposely* passive. This is evident from the fact that in verses 27 and 28 Jesus has used the same verb in the *active voice*. In these verses Jesus referred to the man who *committed* adultery. The passive infinitive of verse 32 refers, however, to the woman who *suffers* adultery. She is "adultered," defamed, disgraced, abused, grievously wronged, debauched (perhaps).

c. The verb is not only *definitely* passive in form, and *purposely* passive in view of the preceding context, but it is *emphatically* passive because it is preceded by *POIEI* ("brings about that," "causes her," "makes her"); hence, "*causes her to suffer adultery,*" or, "*brings about that she suffers adultery.*"

In view of all these considerations it is indeed strange that so many commentators (though by no means all) have failed to see this point.

This having been established, we now proceed to the final clause of the passage in question. Here the verb is also generally translated as an *active*. Notice the following translations:

"And whosoever shall marry her when she is put away *committeth adultery*" (A. R. V.).

"And whosoever shall marry her that is divorced *committeth adultery*" (A. V.).

"And anyone who marries her after she is divorced *commits adultery*" (Goodspeed).

"And whoever marries a divorced woman *commits adultery*" (Moffat).

"En zoo wie de verlatene zal trouwen, *die doet overspel*" (Dutch Staten Vertaling).

"Und wer eine Abgeschiedene freiet, *der bricht die Ehe*" (German).

Over against this common translation and interpretation Lenski advocates a view which is the direct opposite. Instead of making the verb *active*, he would make it *passive* just as in the first part of the passage. Says Lenski, "Here again the *passive* is completely overlooked. This man no more "commits adultery" than the woman "commits adultery." Neither "commits" anything, both have had something committed upon them." Accordingly, Lenski translates as follows, "*and he who shall marry her that has been released is stigmatized as adulterous.*"

Appendix

We disagree with both of these views. The verb should be translated *neither as an active nor as a passive, but as a middle*.

Jesus does *not say* (here in Matthew),
"And whosoever shall marry her that is divorced *committeth adultery*." *Active*.

Neither does he say,
"And whosoever shall marry her that is divorced *suffers adultery* (or: is stigmatized as adulterous). *Passive*.

But he says,
"And he who shall marry her that has been put away *makes himself guilty of adultery*." *Middle*.

We submit the following grounds:

a. The verb certainly is not active in form. If the active had been intended, Matthew could have used it, as is done in the following instances: Matt. 5:27, 28; 19:18; Mk. 10:19; Lk. 16:18; 18:20; Rom. 2:22; 13:9; Jas. 2:11, and Rev. 2:22. In all these cases the translation "to *commit* adultery" is correct. Although Matthew has just used the active, 5:27, 28, he does not do so now. Lenski is correct in observing that the verb is not an active here.

b. Although the active and the middle often resemble each other very closely in meaning, as is the case here (cf. Luke 16:18 where the active is used in a parallel passage), yet *there is a difference*. A. T. Robertson states (and offers abundant proof) that "the only difference between the active and the middle voices is that the middle calls especial attention to the subject. In the active voice the subject is merely acting; in the middle the subject is acting in relation to himself somehow." And Blass remarks, "The N. T. writers were perfectly capable of preserving the distinction between the active and the middle." It will hardly do, therefore, to translate this verb as it occurs in Matt. 5:32 as if it were an active. The verse does not say, "the man who marries the divorced woman *commits adultery*," i. e., it does not direct our attention first of all to the *deed* in the abstract, but it fixes our attention upon this *man*. It says, as it were, "Not only the man who divorced his wife, but also *the one who marries the divorced woman* is guilty. He also *defiles himself; involves himself in sin; makes himself guilty of the sin of adultery*." The verb is plainly not active in form, and should not be translated as an active.

c. As far as the *form* is concerned, it could, of course, be translated as a *passive*. This is what Lenski does. However, his interpretation is at best somewhat far-fetched. The idea would be that the man who marries the divorced woman is still *suffering* because of the sin of her former (i. e., real) husband. The "second" husband does not "commit anything," he is simply *suffering* something. He remains altogether *passive*. But this interpretation loses sight of the parallel passages. In Luke 16:18 we are distinctly told that *"he that marrieth one that is put away from a husband COMMITTETH ADULTERY." The active is used.* Hence, it is very natural to suppose that also in our passage (Matt. 5:32) Jesus looks upon this man who marries the divorced woman as doing something and not *merely as passive*. Moreover, in the other cases where the same *middle* (or passive) *form is used as in Matt 5:32 the meaning, as evident from the context, is plainly not passive but middle. Study for yourself Matt. 19:9; Mk. 10:11; and Mk. 10:12.* In every one of these cases Christ's very clear purpose is to show that the individuals in question *make themselves guilty of* a great sin. They do not merely *suffer* the consequences of someone else's sin. Hence, whereas the identical form of the verb occurs here (Matt. 5:32) in a similar construction, we conclude that the meaning (of the verb) must be the same here as elsewhere. Accordingly, the translation should be:

"But I say unto you that everyone who puts away his wife, saving for the cause of fornication *causes her* (or: is causing her) *to suffer adultery, and he who shall marry her that has been put away makes himself guilty* (or: is making himself guilty) *of adultery."*

On the durative present (present of linear action) see A. T. Robertson, op. cit., p. 879.

www.ingramcontent.com/pod-product-compliance
Lightning Source LLC
Chambersburg PA
CBHW062013220426
43662CB00010B/1309